The Washington Post

DESKBOOK
ON STYLE

The Washington Post

DESKBOOK ON STYLE

Second Edition

COMPILED AND EDITED BY

Thomas W. Lippman

McGraw-Hill Publishing Company

New York   St. Louis   San Francisco   Auckland   Bogotá
Hamburg   London   Madrid   Mexico   Milan   Montreal
New Delhi   Paris   São Paulo   Tokyo   Toronto

2 3 4 5 6 7 8 9 FGR FGR 8 9 2 1 0 9

ISBN 0-07-068414-6

Library of Congress Cataloging-in-Publication Data

The Washington Post deskbook on style.
    Includes index.
    1. Journalism—Style manuals.   2. Washington Post
(1899)   I. Lippman, Thomas W.
PN4783.W35   1989   070.4'15   88-26729
ISBN 0-07-068414-6

Book design by Patrice Fodero

CONTENTS

PREFACE

Words are the raw material of information.

At The Washington Post, reporters and editors process more than 150,000 English words every day, shaping them into sentences, paragraphs, headlines and graphics that convey information about every conceivable subject. That's the equivalent of writing, editing and producing a new 250-page book every 24 hours—a book that is delivered to readers who vary widely in interests, in education levels and in the amount of time they can devote to reading. We insist on accuracy and we strive for clarity. We also want to entertain. The purpose of this stylebook is to provide a consistent and coherent framework for the daunting task of delivering a newspaper that is lively and accessible as well as authoritative.

We strive for fairness and balance in our coverage, and we want to be conscious of the sensitivities of our readers. So in addition to this book's main section, which deals with how we use the English language, you will find here brief essays on our standards and ethics, on newspaper law and libel, on the role of the ombudsman at the newspaper and on the craft of obituary writing. There is also a brief guide to reference materials.

At a newspaper, the word *style* has two meanings: the rules of grammar, punctuation, capitalization and usage that we apply to our written output, and the overall tone or approach. Obviously no single tone or style of writing is appropriate for every article in a publication that reports about every subject, from the cosmic to the trivial, from the tragic to the humorous. Our writing style will change with the material.

But our technical style should not. We are a medium of mass communication. The need to communicate clearly and quickly with a vast and diverse audience imposes its own restrictions. We have little room for Joycean experimentation or 800-word, punctuation-free Faulknerian paragraphs. We strive for consistency of presentation not because we adhere pedantically to inflexible rules but because we want to enlighten our readers. We do not want to confuse them or divert their attention from the material at hand. In addition, we recognize that our newspaper is read every day by students, teachers and scholars who expect us to uphold a high standard of English usage. Consistency of style is part of the high quality they have a right to expect.

In the United States, unlike France, there is no official arbiter of usage. The style that we follow is the style we impose on ourselves, guided by custom, common sense and the scholarship of others. No one can say it is "right" or "wrong" to capitalize the names of Cabinet departments or to omit the comma before the last element in a series. But to the extent that we can be consistent as well as reasonable, we should. It helps the readers, who are our customers, and it shows that we care enough to set a good example for all those to whom we are the most extensive daily contact with the written word.

A newspaper is part of a society's record of itself. Each day's edition lives on in libraries and electronic archives, to be consulted again and again by the scholars and journalists of the future. The newspaper is thus a repository of the language, and we have a responsibility to treat the language with respect. The rules of grammar, punctuation, capitalization, spelling and usage set down here are our way of trying to meet that responsibility.

Compilation of this stylebook was a collaborative effort. The task could not have been accomplished without substantial contributions from my colleagues Richard Harwood, Pat Myers, Marcia Kramer and Tom Dimond. I also received invaluable assistance from Keith Sinzinger, Curt Hazlett, Richard Pearson, Joyce Murdoch, Karen Turley, John Sharkey, Edward B. Purcell, Richard Furno, Herb Pierson, Bill Broadway, Judith Havemann, Donald Beard, Sandra Bailey and Robert A. Webb. They deserve much of the credit for what is valuable in this stylebook. Responsibility for its deficiencies lies with me.

Thomas W. Lippman
March 1989

CHAPTER 1

STANDARDS AND ETHICS

Benjamin C. Bradlee

The Washington Post is pledged to an aggressive, responsible and fair pursuit of the truth without fear of any special interest, and with favor to none.

Washington Post reporters and editors are pledged to approach every assignment with the fairness of open minds and without prior judgment. The search for opposing views must be routine. Comment from persons accused or challenged in stories must be included. The motives of those who press their views upon us must routinely be examined, and it must be recognized that those motives can be noble or ignoble, obvious or ulterior.

We fully recognize that the power we have inherited as the dominant morning newspaper in the capital of the free world carries with it special responsibilities:

- to listen to the voiceless.

Benjamin C. Bradlee is executive editor of The Washington Post.

- to avoid any and all acts of arrogance.
- to face the public politely and candidly.

Conflict of Interest

This newspaper is pledged to avoid conflict of interest or the appearance of conflict of interest, wherever and whenever possible. We have adopted stringent policies on these issues, conscious that they may be more restrictive than is customary in the world of private business. In particular:

- We pay our own way.
- We accept no gifts from news sources. We accept no free trips. We neither seek nor accept preferential treatment that might be rendered because of the positions we hold. Exceptions to the no-gift rule are few and obvious—invitations to meals, for example, may be accepted when they are occasional and innocent, but not when they are repeated and their purpose is deliberately calculating. Free admissions to any event that is not free to the public are prohibited. The only exception is for seats not sold to the public, as in a press box. Whenever possible, arrangements will be made to pay for such seats.
- We work for no one except The Washington Post without permission from supervisors. Many outside activities and jobs are incompatible with the proper performance of work on an independent newspaper. Connections with government are among the most objectionable. To avoid real or apparent conflicts of interest in the coverage of business and the financial markets, all members of the Business and Financial staff are required to disclose their financial holdings and investments to the assistant managing editor in charge of the section. The potential for conflict, however, is not limited to members of the Business and Financial staff. All

reporters and editors, wherever they may work, are required to disclose to their department head any financial interests that might be in conflict or give the appearance of a conflict in their reporting or editing duties. Department heads will make their own financial disclosures to the managing editor.

• We freelance for no one and accept no speaking engagements without permission from department heads. Permission to freelance will be granted only if The Post has no interest in the story and only if it is to appear in a medium that does not compete with The Post. It is important that no freelance assignments and no honoraria be accepted that might in any way be interpreted as disguised gratuities.

• We make every reasonable effort to be free of obligation to news sources and to special interests. We must be wary of entanglement with those whose positions render them likely to be subjects of journalistic interest and examination. Our private behavior as well as our professional behavior must not bring discredit to our profession or to The Post.

• We avoid active involvement in any partisan causes—politics, community affairs, social action, demonstrations—that could compromise or seem to compromise our ability to report and edit fairly. Relatives cannot fairly be made subject to Post rules, but it should be recognized that their employment or their involvement in causes can at least appear to compromise our integrity. The business and professional ties of traditional family members or other members of your household must be disclosed to department heads.

The Reporter's Role

Although it has become increasingly difficult for this newspaper and for the press generally to do so since Watergate, reporters should make every effort to remain in the audience, to be the stagehand rather than the star, to report the news, not to make the news.

In gathering news, reporters will not misrepresent their identity. They will not identify themselves as police officers, physicians or anything other than journalists.

Errors

This newspaper is pledged to minimize the number of errors we make and to correct those that occur. Accuracy is our goal; candor is our defense. Persons who call errors to our attention must be accorded a respectful hearing. See Chapter 3, "The Role of the Ombudsman."

Attribution of Sources

The Washington Post is pledged to disclose the source of all information when at all possible. When we agree to protect a source's identity, that identity will not be made known to anyone outside The Post.

Before any information is accepted without full attribution, reporters must make every reasonable effort to get it on the record. If that is not possible, reporters should consider seeking the information elsewhere. If that in turn is not possible, reporters should request an on-the-record reason for concealing the source's identity and should include the reason in the story.

In any case, some kind of identification is almost always possible—by department or by position, for example—and should be reported.

No pseudonyms are to be used. See PSEUDONYMS in Chapter 5.

However, The Washington Post will not knowingly disclose the identities of U.S. intelligence agents, except under highly unusual circumstances which must be weighed by the senior editors.

Plagiarism and Credit

Attribution of material from other newspapers and other media must be total. Plagiarism is one of journalism's unforgivable sins. It is the policy of this newspaper to give credit to other publications that develop exclusive stories worthy of coverage by The Post.

Fairness

Reporters and editors of The Post are committed to fairness. While arguments about objectivity are endless, the concept of fairness is something that editors and reporters can easily understand and pursue. Fairness results from a few simple practices·

- No story is fair if it omits facts of major importance or significance. Fairness includes completeness.
- No story is fair if it includes essentially irrelevant information at the expense of significant facts. Fairness includes relevance.
- No story is fair if it consciously or unconsciously misleads or even deceives the reader. Fairness includes honesty—leveling with the reader.
- No story is fair if reporters hide their biases or emotions behind such subtly pejorative words as "refused," "despite," "quietly," "admit" and "massive." Fairness requires straightforwardness ahead of flashiness.

Opinion

On this newspaper, the separation of news columns from the editorial and opposite-editorial pages is solemn and complete. This separation is intended to serve the reader, who is entitled to the facts in the news columns and to opinions on the editorial and "op-ed" pages. But nothing in this separation of functions is intended to eliminate from the news columns honest, in-depth reporting, or analysis or commentary when plainly labeled.

The National and Community Interest

The Washington Post is vitally concerned with the national interest and with the community interest. We believe these interests are best served by the widest possible dissemination of information. The claim of national interest by a federal official does not automatically equate with the national interest. The claim of community interest by a local official does not automatically equate with the community interest.

Taste

The Washington Post as a newspaper respects taste and decency, understanding that society's concepts of taste and decency are constantly changing. A word offensive to the last generation can be part of the next generation's common vocabulary. But we shall avoid prurience. We shall avoid profanities and obscenities unless their use is so essential to a story of significance that its meaning is lost without them. In no case shall obscenities be used without the approval of the executive editor or the managing editor or his deputy. See Chapter 5, "Using the Language," for guidance on particular words or terms that may be sensitive.

The Post's Principles

After Eugene Meyer bought The Washington Post in 1933 and began the family ownership that continues today, he published "These Principles":

THE FIRST MISSION OF A NEWSPAPER IS TO TELL THE TRUTH AS NEARLY AS THE TRUTH MAY BE ASCERTAINED.

THE NEWSPAPER SHALL TELL ALL THE TRUTH SO FAR AS IT CAN LEARN IT, CONCERNING THE IMPORTANT AFFAIRS OF AMERICA AND THE WORLD.

AS A DISSEMINATOR OF THE NEWS, THE PAPER SHALL OBSERVE THE DECENCIES THAT ARE OBLIGATORY UPON A PRIVATE GENTLE-MAN.

WHAT IT PRINTS SHALL BE FIT READING FOR THE YOUNG AS WELL AS FOR THE OLD.

THE NEWSPAPER'S DUTY IS TO ITS READERS AND TO THE PUBLIC AT LARGE, AND NOT TO THE PRIVATE INTERESTS OF THE OWNER.

IN THE PURSUIT OF TRUTH, THE NEWSPAPER SHALL BE PREPARED TO MAKE SACRIFICES OF ITS MATERIAL FORTUNES, IF SUCH COURSE BE NECESSARY FOR THE PUBLIC GOOD. THE NEWSPAPER SHALL NOT BE THE ALLY OF ANY SPECIAL INTEREST, BUT SHALL BE FAIR AND FREE AND WHOLESOME IN ITS OUTLOOK ON PUBLIC AFFAIRS AND PUBLIC MEN.

"These Principles" are re-endorsed herewith.

CHAPTER 2

LEGAL ISSUES

Boisfeuillet Jones Jr.

Libel

Libel, a published false statement that harms someone's reputation, is the grim reaper of loose journalism. Libel can be devastating to the subject, and an ensuing suit can be debilitating for the reporter. Aside from the newspaper's legal costs and potential exposure to large damage awards, libel suits can drain time and morale in the newsroom.

If the newspaper is to inform the public about controversial matters, it must expect the occasional libel suit. People sue not only to vindicate an injustice to reputation, but also to intimidate and deter, punish, bolster a defense of rectitude in another proceeding, or dip into a deep pocket. And some people in the public eye who are familiar with courts—police, developers, prosecutors, lawyers —do not hesitate to sue.

Boisfeuillet Jones Jr. is general counsel of The Washington Post.

Familiarity with libel law should cause neither timidity nor irresponsibility. It can reduce the risk of litigation and promote accuracy and fairness. But the law provides no simple formulas, often changes, and varies from state to state. This stylebook section is not intended to provide rules or guidelines. Generally, the best way to avoid libel problems is through sound journalism and a sense of fairness. Counsel should be consulted about legal concerns.

HARM TO REPUTATION

To be libelous, a statement must injure reputation ("defame") or otherwise cause actual injury. Whether a statement is defamatory depends upon the entire context and reasonable implications, not just literal language.

Although discredit or contempt in the community—rather than mere annoyance to the subject—is theoretically necessary, courts often have let suits proceed over almost any disparaging statement about a person, private entity, or product. Harm may be presumed if the statement denigrates someone's integrity (by suggesting criminal conduct or dishonesty), skills (professional incompetence), or business (insolvency).

Since harm is required to establish libel, the statement must be made to someone other than the person or organization claiming to be defamed, and the complainant must be identifiable from the statement. A person may be identifiable without being explicitly named, if part of the community can recognize the individual from the article.

A reporter can incur liability for slander (the oral equivalent of libel) by spreading allegations to third persons during interviews. Checking the accuracy of allegations or rumors is part of a reporter's job, but it calls for care in framing questions.

FALSITY

A true statement, even if injurious, cannot be libelous. Substantial truth is what the law requires. However, persons who cannot dispute the basic, stinging facts still sometimes sue over small errors in an attempt to discredit the entire article. The grievant's lawyer, looking for a point of weakness wherever one can be found, will claim that erroneous details are themselves damaging and indicative of careless or biased journalism. Complaints of falsity may arise not only from what is explicitly stated, but also from what is suggested or implied. The implication can be created by the omission of significant facts. Or it can be an oblique reference to an incidental person or questionable matter in an accusatory story.

Headlines, leads, and cutlines can present problems. By trying to capture the gist of the article in a compressed way, they may be unintentionally overstated or misstated. A person may sue for being misquoted, if the inaccuracy harms reputation. One reason for reporters to preserve interview notes for a reasonable period is to minimize disputes over what was said.

Printing a false statement made by someone else can itself be libelous even if the newspaper neutrally attributes the statement without indicating that it is true. This principle of libel law—referred to as the republication rule—is often misunderstood. When the newspaper quotes a source who has made a libelous statement, the newspaper has republished the libelous statement. It cannot defend a libel suit on the ground of truth if the underlying statement turns out to be false. Of course, other defenses still may be available.

FAULT

As constitutional law now stands—and this is libel's main battleground—some degree of fault by the press (or any other speaker) must be proved. Historically under state law, one was strictly liable for making a defamatory falsehood no matter how much care had been exercised. However, the rise in libel cases involving potentially ruinous damage awards threatened to discourage speech about provocative news.

The Supreme Court of the United States, beginning with the *New York Times v. Sullivan* decision in 1964, set levels of fault necessary to sustain a claim of libel, depending on whether the statements were about public officials and public figures, or about private individuals.

Those who have assumed a role of general prominence in society, or who have injected themselves into a public controversy that is being written about, are treated as public figures. Others who do not fall into these categories may also be treated as public figures. It is often difficult to predict whether an individual or organization will be treated as a public figure (or official), given illogical conclusions reached by some courts.

The public figure or public official must show what is confusingly called "actual malice"—that is, knowledge of falsity or reckless disregard of the truth. Another way of stating the test is that the complainant must prove that the reporter seriously doubted the truth of the statement or realized that it was probably false. The complainant's lawyer may attempt to prove actual malice by arguing there were obvious reasons to doubt the veracity of a news source or the accuracy of the source's charges.

The private figure must show at least negligence—that is, a failure to exercise reasonable care in ascertaining and publishing the truth. The complainant's lawyer will try to show that a reasonably careful journalist would have done something more to verify what was published or would have been more careful in guarding against unfounded defamatory implications.

Liability cannot be established by claiming that an article is not balanced, but as a practical matter any apparent unfairness may precipitate a lawsuit. Conversely, balance and fairness—including the publication of the response of one who is the subject of an allegation—will deter suits and strengthen any defense.

The ability to cite reliable sources may be important to a defense under any fault standard. If a reporter bases a statement on absolutely confidential sources—who have been promised they will not be named as sources even if the newspaper is sued for libel—persuading the judge or jury that there was an adequate basis for the article may be difficult.

OFFICIAL PROCEEDINGS

The laws of every state and the District of Columbia provide a privilege to publish accounts of official reports and proceedings. The purpose of the privilege is to enable the public to be informed about government affairs and conduct. The privilege is applied most frequently to protect coverage of judicial proceedings, but it also applies to articles on legislative, executive, and other official proceedings and actions such as arrests. It applies to official reports, such as those of a Congressional committee or a Cabinet department's inspector general.

The privilege may be unavailable if the article does not clearly refer to the official report or proceeding as the source for the statement. Attribution enables the reader to understand the context of an allegation and negates an implication that the newspaper is originating or crediting it.

The privilege does not apply to statements made outside the course of the official proceeding, such as interviews with prosecutors or police who are commenting on an arrest. The privilege does not protect reporting that is inaccurate or unfairly taken out of context. Direct quotes or close paraphrases can often avoid problems that might result from imprecise characterizations or incorrect interpretations. Although not always practical, review of documents avoids the risk of relying on sources to relay the contents, a risk that is compounded if the source then denies giving the information incorrectly.

Focusing on only an isolated part of a record may place a statement in an unfair context. For example, a damaging assertion may be qualified or retracted a few paragraphs later in a transcript; arrests and charges may have been dismissed or otherwise disposed of; or the facts stated in a court opinion may not be findings at all, but rather a recitation of the allegations or facts assumed to be true solely for purposes of ruling on the particular motion.

Unless names and identifying details are omitted, use of a pending case to illustrate some type of misconduct featured in an article (sexual harassment, child abuse, stock fraud) requires care to avoid an implication of guilt.

While publishing a response to allegations may not be legally required, especially if a response is not part of the record, obtaining a response from the accused will enable readers to know that the allegations are in dispute, and what (if anything) the other side has to say. Reaching the accused for comment may also help avoid damaging errors such as misstating charges and mistaking identity between similarly named people.

NEUTRAL REPORTAGE

Some courts have recognized a separate privilege of neutral reportage, which protects fair and balanced reporting of newsworthy charges made by responsible individuals or organizations about public officials and public figures. The rationale for the privilege is that sometimes the mere fact that a charge has been made is newsworthy and should be reported, regardless of the reporter's belief in its truth.

To invoke the privilege, a publisher will want to demonstrate that the charges were presented in a neutral fashion, without advocacy of their validity, that the subject's denial was also given prominence, and that the report was generally a balanced one. Not all state courts have had occasion to pass upon the existence of this privilege. Not all of those who have had the opportunity have recognized it. And not all allegations will be covered by the privilege even when it is recognized. However, presenting charges neutrally and including the subject's response may enable counsel to urge the applicability of this privilege in the event of a lawsuit.

OPINION

Expressions of opinion are protected. But the line between fact and opinion is not easily drawn. One test is whether a statement is capable of being proved true or false, or rather reflects a subjective judgment upon which people may differ. Labeling a statement "opinion" may be helpful, but does not necessarily buy protection. Editorial and opinion pages contain factual material, and the news pages of any newspaper contain statements that the law regards as opinion. News articles may contain expressions of opinions attributed to news sources, or they may reflect the reporter's own assessment or analysis, explicit or implicit, of a particular set of facts. A statement of opinion may be more identifiable as such if it is accompanied by a statement of its factual basis. Political cartoons, although not necessarily immune, are usually ruled to be protected as obvious hyperbole or exaggerated symbols.

Colorful quotes often contain expressions of opinion that are legally protected but stir resentment nevertheless. Including a response from the person criticized, in addition to being fair, will often as a practical matter lessen the risk of suit. High officials and politicians, as part of public debate, expect a certain amount of invective and rhetoric. Restaurants, shows, sports figures, entertainers and others who invite public attention can expect criticism, as long as it is targeted on the cuisine, entertainment value, athletic performance, or whatever else is being offered to the public.

HANDLING COMPLAINTS

Demands for corrections should be handled politely, fairly, and quickly. It is important both to check out disputed details and to look at the entire context rather than mere technical error. In an undefensive manner the person handling the call should listen carefully to the caller's side of the story, agree to get back in touch, and inform an editor.

When someone mentions libel, threatens a lawsuit, or has a lawyer call the newspaper, the caller should be referred to counsel for all communications. Statements uttered to a complainant might be usable in a later suit.

Errors are corrected regardless of threats. But often the complaint relates to an ambiguous matter, alleged implication, or incomplete treatment of one side. These may call for a clarification, follow-up article, letter or other response which the newspaper will want handled with an awareness of possible litigation.

Privacy

Encroachments on an individual's privacy produce more indignation than litigation. Nevertheless, for a newspaper widely read in the community, sensitivity is important. Basic decency and common sense in gathering information and in deciding what to publish will avoid liability for several types of invasion of privacy recognized to a varying extent among the states.

INTRUSION

Intrusion into a person's seclusion or private affairs may occur in the course of newsgathering, even if nothing is ever published. Whether conduct amounts to intrusion will depend upon the particular circumstances. Examples of what may amount to this type of invasion of privacy are: entering a person's home or hotel room without permission, breaking into an office, electronically eavesdropping on a conversation, opening a person's mail, or gaining access to an individual's bank records by misrepresentation. Recording a telephone conversation with a source, without the source's consent, may violate the law of some states (e.g., Maryland) and result in a privacy complaint.

If a third person through intrusion obtains information and later provides it to a reporter, the newspaper may publish it without liability for intrusion unless the newspaper induced the intrusion. Obtaining the individual's consent is the best way to avoid potential claims of intrusion. When consent is unavailable in sensitive situations, reporters and photographers should consult with their editor and with counsel, if practicable.

PERSONAL INFORMATION

Outrage at newspapers' publication of highly personal facts led to the development of a right of privacy. Truth is not at issue; the questions are whether the matter disclosed is private, whether it is newsworthy, and whether the disclosure would be highly offensive to a reasonable person.

These judgments are subjective, requiring an editor to assess the public interest in knowing the information and to balance it against the individual's privacy interest. Often the question boils down to how much detail should be published. Not surprisingly, legal rulings provide no consistent guidance on whether something is of general interest or is highly offensive to an ordinary person. In the case of a public figure, the public's legitimate interest may include matters that would otherwise be private.

As a matter of constitutional law, a privacy claim cannot arise from publication of names and details from open public records and proceedings. But this right does not mean that the newspaper will choose to publish such information when it is gratuitous or of minimal general interest.

One way to avoid problems with private facts is to omit an individual's name and other identifying information from the article. But this measure is not feasible in many situations, and in other situations the use of names, although not absolutely necessary, can personalize and add credibility to the article. There are no absolute rules in this area, but newspapers as a general matter do not publish the names of surviving victims of sex crimes, the names of juveniles charged in juvenile court, or embarrassing facts of no current news value from someone's distant past.

Use of photographs can follow the guideline of reasonable expectations. People who can be seen from public places without telescopic lenses—people on a street, in a park, in an arrest or an accident, or in the front yard of a home—generally have no expectation of privacy. A photograph in a public place may be a problem only if the subject is caught in a very embarrassing moment of no news value (e.g., skirt lifted by gust of wind).

Consent is a complete defense to a privacy claim. For children and incompetents, consent is ordinarily obtained from the parent or guardian. A minor may have the capacity to give consent if the individual is mature enough to appreciate the significance of what is published. The subject of a proposed story may withdraw or limit consent prior to publication—a legal rule instinctively difficult for journalists, who know they usually have no obligation to put an on-the-record statement off the record when the source has second thoughts.

Sometimes it is advisable to obtain a written release, preferably in the presence of a witness. For example, a school for retarded children may obtain written releases from parents allowing photographs at the school. Any consent should make clear that the information or photograph is to be published in the newspaper.

FALSE LIGHT

A privacy claim may arise if a person is falsely associated with something objectionable. "False light" is very similar to libel, except that injury to reputation need not be shown. Sometimes a misquote or omission of crucial facts from an article causes an embarrassing and offensive misimpression.

Claims most typically arise from use of a photograph out of context to illustrate an unflattering feature article unrelated to the individual. Examples are a photograph of women on a street corner to accompany a story on prostitution, and a photograph of men on a street corner to accompany a story on unemployment or drug distribution. Shadowing of faces may make individuals unidentifiable.

MISAPPROPRIATION

Exploitation of a person's name or likeness for commercial gain, without permission, is misappropriation. Use of names and photographs in news articles is generally protected from liability under this theory, but a newsroom is rightfully wary of requests to re-use photographs for advertisements, endorsements, and non-news products.

National Security

A newspaper in the nation's capital has dual responsibilities in reporting on security matters—to exercise caution in handling sensitive information, and to report beyond a less-than-candid official line on significant policy matters. Editors balance the public interest in knowing information against the possibility of damage to the nation's security.

Unauthorized disclosures, or "leaks," of government secrets by the executive and legislative branches are part of daily coverage of defense, intelligence, and diplomatic matters. Leaks—to promote or discredit policies, to defend or expose practices, to ingratiate— have for better or worse become part of the system of accountability and self-governance.

The fact that information is or is not classified, while significant, is not necessarily dispositive of whether the information should be published. Over-classification is rampant, and highly sensitive information such as planned military tactics in the field may not always be classified. Congress has not outlawed unauthorized disclosure of information merely because it is classified. Laws do prohibit disclosure of information regarding certain matters—atomic energy data, communications intelligence and intercepts, codes, and lists of covert agents' names. And where the government asserts that publication may jeopardize national security, it may threaten prosecution of the press under espionage laws or even under the law prohibiting theft or conversion of government property.

The newspaper often engages in a dialogue with the government about what it intends to publish. The newspaper may consult knowledgeable authorities as well as listen to agency spokesmen (or higher officials if they consider the matter to be sufficiently important) on the potential impact of disclosure. Experience has shown that potential harm is sometimes greatly exaggerated to discourage disclosure of politically embarrassing information. Nevertheless, editors pay careful attention when the government explains its objections in other than highly speculative terms.

Subpoenas

Journalists, as a result of what they publish, are from time to time subpoenaed in third-party suits to testify about what they were told while gathering news. Their testimony may be useful to a litigant, but it will intrude on the editorial process and may discourage sources from talking freely with a reporter in the future for fear that their remarks will end up in court.

To promote the free flow of information to the public and to protect the editorial process, most courts have recognized a qualified privilege protecting reporters from testifying about newsgathering unless the information sought is central to the case and cannot be obtained by alternative means. The state's interests in law enforcement and a defendant's right to a fair trial may override the privilege in criminal proceedings. Shield laws in some states (including Maryland) provide varying degrees of additional protection from subpoenas.

The Post will first try to discourage lawyers from subpoenaing reporters and photographers. If that fails, The Post will assert the privilege in court. If ultimately ordered to testify, the journalist will have to testify or be held in contempt of court.

A reporter who is contacted by a lawyer involved in a case should simply refer the matter to The Post's counsel. Any discussion with the lawyer about the journalist's memory, notes, or photographs will make the problem more difficult.

Prior Restraint, Fair Trial

Judicial orders to stop a publication are rare in the case of "pure" speech—as opposed to copyrighted material, obscene material and commercial speech like advertising. Prior restraints on news are permitted, if at all, only in extraordinary circumstances such as a compelling matter of national security.

Nevertheless, judges occasionally issue restraining orders that, intentionally or not, apply to the newspaper. Refusal to comply will result in contempt if the order is later upheld. As a general rule even improper orders must be obeyed, but there may be a right to disregard a transparently invalid order infringing First Amendment rights. Counsel should be alerted immediately concerning such an order, so that appropriate relief may be speedily sought from a higher court.

Restraints most frequently become an issue when press coverage of criminal proceedings seems to threaten a defendant's right to a fair trial. Since direct restraints on the press have been invalidated, judges instead may issue "gag" orders on trial participants to prevent prejudicial publicity.

Ethical codes also limit what prosecutors and attorneys may say to the press about a pending proceeding. In general, there is no problem obtaining their comment on the nature of the charges and the defense, the status of an investigation, the circumstances of an arrest, the identity of the victim, and what evidence was seized. The difficulty is with comments suggestive of guilt—reciting police records, characterizing the defendant's reputation or the likelihood of guilt, using the word "confession" or "admission" rather than "statement," noting a failure to make a statement, or predicting a possible plea bargain. A reporter who has questions about the propriety of such a quote should consult a senior editor.

Sensitivity to fair trial considerations is particularly important after jury selection has begun. Close questioning of potential jurors by the judge can effectively screen out possible prejudice up to that time. Courts will sometimes admonish reporters about publicizing incriminating matters not admissible during the trial. In these situations editors will have to weigh this consideration against the importance of conveying the information to the public at the time it is most interested in the trial.

Copyright and Trademark

COPYRIGHT

The copyright statute protects owners of photographs and writings from unauthorized copying by others. The law protects the manner of expression, not the information itself. Works of the government, such as documents published by the Government Printing Office, are in the public domain. A notice of copyright and registration at the Copyright Office are not necessary to protect the owner, but may affect the extent of the owner's remedy.

A "fair use" defense may justify verbatim lifting of limited portions of a work to convey its ideas or style, such as in a book review or article about a newsworthy revelation in a book. The fair use defense may not apply at all to preemptive use of excerpts of an unpublished manuscript prior to its release for first publication by the author. One consideration in determining whether a use is "fair" is whether it will hurt the market value of the work.

TRADEMARK

Trade names should be used only as a proper adjective or noun in conjunction with a particular product or service (e.g., Xerox copier) and not in lowercase or otherwise as a generally descriptive word (e.g., as a verb).

Trademark owners or their attorneys write to complain about generic use and to seek assurance it will not happen again. Their letters should be forwarded to counsel for acknowledgment.

A trademark holder's vigilance is necessary as a technical, legal matter to defend against claims from competitors that the trade name has been sufficiently diluted to come within the public domain for any product to use—as occurred with words like "aspirin," "yo-

yo," "nylon," "escalator" and "thermos." See TRADE NAMES AND BRANDS in Chapter 5.

Access to Courts

Court secrecy has become an increasingly frustrating problem for reporters, even though judicial proceedings and records are presumptively open. Generally, a judge should find "good cause" before closing a hearing or sealing a record. The justification for closure must be particularly compelling in criminal proceedings, including those at the pre-trial stage. Judges usually recognize the right of the press and public to intervene in proceedings in order to request access. However, the absence of advance notice of court closures can create practical problems. The remedy of access to a transcript later may be inadequate because of the diminished news value and the cost of the transcript. If at the outset of a proceeding a judge is considering barring the press and public, the reporter should immediately seek permission to address the court in order (1) to assert the right to be present in court as a common-law and constitutional right, and (2) to request a short adjournment so that the reporter's attorney can be heard on the issue. Alerting an editor and counsel at the first opportunity is obviously crucial.

Bench conferences, in which opposing counsel in a court case confer with the judge out of the hearing of the jury and the public, create similar practical problems of timeliness. The newspaper may during trials ask judges to refrain from repeatedly holding bench conferences when the jury is not present.

If a reporter wants to inspect records that have been used in court but are sealed, counsel should be consulted about intervening in the case to file a motion to unseal. Not all material or testimony provided to a party during the discovery process in a lawsuit is filed in court, and there may be no public right of access to such material.

A party may still elect to make them available unless the judge has placed them under a protective order for a specified reason.

Access to Government

RECORDS

The Freedom of Information Act (FOIA) and similar state laws require that government agencies provide public access to their records unless a specific exemption applies. The most common exemptions include properly classified information; internal personnel practices; information expressly exempted by another statute; trade secrets and privileged business data; internal deliberative memoranda; personnel, medical, and other records that invade personal privacy; certain investigatory material compiled for law enforcement purposes; and many regulatory reports on financial institutions. If a record is not completely exempt, the agency is required to make available non-exempt portions that are reasonably separable.

Disputes often arise about whether certain data are beyond the scope of the FOIA. The FOIA defines "agencies" to include executive departments, military departments, the executive office of the President (but not the White House staff), government-controlled corporations, and independent government regulatory agencies. Congress and the federal courts are not covered by the law. "Records" are documents, tapes, microfilm and other forms of data compilation within the agency's possession or control. An agency is not required to create documents.

A sample letter of request is on page 27. The description of the requested records should be specific enough to permit a reasonable search, but inclusive enough to preclude circumvention by the agency through a narrow interpretation. A clean copy of the request should be preserved for use in case of appeal or litigation. It may be helpful for counsel to handle an appeal.

Federal and local agencies vary widely in being responsive to requests. Knowing that newspapers may lose their interest if timely release does not occur, agencies can drag out the process to avoid disclosure of embarrassing records. Follow-up calls can sometimes help.

MEETINGS

Federal and state "sunshine acts" require that certain government meetings be open to the public if decisions are being made. These laws are useful in requiring advance announcement of the time, location, and subject matter of certain meetings, as well as the name of a contact person for background documents and information. The Federal Register publishes most notices at least a week before federal agency meetings. Generally, covered meetings are those at which a quorum is present and able to take action on behalf of the agency.

Agencies may close meetings, or portions of them, when it is likely the meetings will fall within a number of categories, including the same general areas (personnel, deliberative, etc.) exempt under the public records laws. Meetings typically may be closed only by a recorded majority vote, with a written statement of reasons and list of persons expected to attend. Transcripts or, in some cases, minutes are usually required to be kept and must be made available except for exempt portions.

While open-meetings laws are easy and tempting for officials to circumvent—who wants to discuss sensitive matters candidly in public, when it can be done over lunch?—raising objections can sometimes embarrass the agency into sticking to the formalities.

An editor and counsel should be notified as soon as the reporter learns a meeting will be closed for no apparently adequate reason. Most laws allow courts to stop a meeting pending a decision on closure, and closures may also be challenged later (within time limits) to gain access to the transcript or minutes.

Sample Letter Requesting Federal Agency Records

Dear (person designated in agency regulations):

Pursuant to the Freedom of Information Act, 5 U.S.C. 552, as amended, I hereby request disclosure of the following records for inspection and possible copying: [List documents, with identifying descriptions, as fully and specifically as possible].

If you regard any records in the foregoing list as exempt from required disclosure under the Act, I hereby request that you exercise your discretion to disclose them nevertheless.

I further request that you disclose the listed documents as they become available to you, without waiting until all the documents have been assembled.

I am making this request on behalf of The Washington Post, a newspaper of general circulation in the Washington, D.C., metropolitan area and the United States. The records disclosed pursuant to this request will be used in preparing news articles for dissemination to the public. Accordingly, I request that, pursuant to 5 U.S.C. 552(a) (4) (A), you waive all fees in the public interest because the furnishing of the requested information will primarily benefit the public. However, if you decline to waive all fees, I am prepared to pay your normal search fees (and copying fees if I decide to copy any records), but I request that you notify me if you expect your search fees to exceed $_____.

I look forward to hearing from you promptly.

Sincerely,

CHAPTER 3

THE ROLE OF THE OMBUDSMAN

Richard Harwood

There are approximately 1,750 daily newspapers in the United States, many of them mom-and-pop operations owned by absentee corporations. All of them have publishers, press crews, editors, reporters and advertising salespeople. But only 35 or so of our daily newspapers employ "ombudsmen" or their counterparts who carry such titles as "Readers' Advocate," "Reader Representative" or "Readers' Contact Editor."

The first of these functionaries appeared in 1967 at the Louisville Courier-Journal. His assignment was to deal with customer complaints about all aspects of the newspaper's operations, from delivery service to editorial policies. This pioneer was an "inside" operator, meaning that he served only as a conduit between customers and various managers at the newspaper. He did not independently evaluate and critique the newspaper's performance, nor did he publish

Richard Harwood, formerly deputy managing editor of The Washington Post, is the newspaper's ombudsman.

confessions of error or moralistic sermons on the sinfulness of our trade.

The Washington Post was next, getting into the business of ombudsmanship in 1970. It shaped the function according to its own needs. The ombudsman (who did not then carry that awkward title, a Swedish word meaning representative) dealt with the public only on problems involving the newsroom. But he acted independently in circulating frequent memoranda on what seemed to him to be the newspaper's shortcomings and in publishing from time to time a "News Business" column on the editorial page.

The ombudsman's function at The Post is roughly the same today and to a considerable extent has become a model for other newspapers. Most ombudsmen and "reader advocates," for example, now publish columns explaining why and how certain decisions are made, expressing contrition for errors and, on occasion, taking the institution to task for clumsiness, incompetence or other frailties.

Each year the ranks of ombudsmen expand by one or two, indicating that the office is probably here to stay. There are two other important survival indicators: A national Organization of Newspaper Ombudsmen has been created, and at least one newspaper at an Ivy League university, the Daily Princetonian, has become a convert to the movement.

The motives of newspaper editors and publishers in creating house critics and inspectors-general no doubt have been quite mixed. Some owners—the Binghams of Louisville, for example—seem to have acted out of a patrician sense of community responsibility. Their communications company was a local monopoly accountable, in effect, to no one but themselves. An ombudsman, they believed, would alert them to real or imagined abuses of power and acts of arrogance on the part of the newspaper and would, perhaps, provide lines of communication between the institution and voiceless or ignored elements of the community.

This ethic of community responsibility was a factor in The Washington Post's decision to be "responsive" to its readers and indulge in self-criticism. There were clear pressures from the marketplace as well. The paper, during the years of turmoil in the late 1960s and early 1970s, was a lightning rod for the passions of the times and a frequent target of Agnew-ites seeking to make of the "Eastern Liberal Press" a scapegoat for the erosion of traditional values. Popular dissatisfaction with the newspaper in those days of turbulence and rage was reflected in a substantial attrition of the subscription lists. It also provided, here and elsewhere, an outpouring of soul-searching and self-examination by media institutions of all description. This in turn, I suspect, nourished the growth of the ombudsman movement.

From the beginning the movement has had a substantial public relations dimension. The gesture is encapsulated in the advertising theme of the Giant Food supermarket chain: "We care about YOU." But it has not been, in my experience, a noticeably hollow or deceptive gesture. Ombudsmen at The Post and elsewhere act, for the most part, in the public interest as best they perceive it. Their triumphs are modest, not revolutionary. For the reader, they often serve the function of the Army chaplain: I may not solve your problem but I'll listen to you talk about it and try to make you feel better.

Ombudsmen have another utility. Editors in large metropolitan newsrooms rarely have unused blocks of time for what might be called "customer relations." Their calendars are filled with meetings. The budgets over which they preside are measured in the tens of millions of dollars and they are expected by their companies to be good managers. They employ hundreds of people whose personal and professional problems and quirks have endless permutations— all of them, it sometimes appears, requiring the personal attention of the editor. Ombudsmen provide these newsroom managers with another set of skeptical eyes to search out human error and incompetence and another set of ears to lend to the masses. The editor may not be able to respond personally to a complaint or suggestion, but there is someone to whom he can forward the letter or refer the call.

These eyes and ears most often belong to ombudsmen or "advocates" who are regular employees of the newspaper, employees who are very often long in the tooth—senior citizens, so to speak. The Post too chose in-house ombudsmen in the early 1970s but thereafter, with one exception, has gone outside the newspaper to hire on contract people with backgrounds in journalism or public affairs. These contracts insulate the ombudsman from internal interference and guarantee his independence.

It is proper to ask whether ombudsmen, as independent or semi-independent operators, accomplish anything worth accomplishing. Do they "improve" the newspapers that employ them or act beneficially on the business of journalism in general? These are the sorts of questions reporters and editors obsessively ask themselves. Does our work make any difference, or are our impact and influence pure illusion? We comfort ourselves, sometimes, by saying that while we may not tell people what to think, we are often successful in telling them what to think about. Ombudsmen do that with editors. We make them think about their audiences, their standards and the quality of their journalism. That is all an ombudsman should expect. He is not God; he is not even one of the angels.

CHAPTER 4

THE CRAFT OF THE OBITUARY

J. Y. Smith

The occasion for obituaries is death, which is sad. But the subject of obituaries is life itself, which is wonderful. Obituaries are the news stories that bring The Washington Post into the closest and most intimate contact with its readers, and they are among the most sensitive stories the newspaper publishes.

Unlike other newspapers, The Washington Post guarantees to publish the obituary of anyone who has been a longtime or permanent resident of the Washington area. We initiate news obituaries about public figures whose lives we think are of general interest. We also publish obituaries about private citizens if their families request it and provide enough information. There is democracy in death and we respect it, provided the families of the deceased are willing to give us what we need. But obtaining this information is often the source of difficulty.

The hardest part of obituary work is taking telephone calls from

J. Y. Smith was obituary editor of The Washington Post from 1977 to 1988.

grieving, confused people. Whatever happens, callers must be treated sympathetically. Remember that the average caller has had no previous contact with newspaper reporters and may not understand the purpose of our questions. Most problems can be resolved by explaining what the newspaper can and cannot do. The cardinal rule is to be accurate, sympathetic, firm and consistent. The paper cannot be in the position of handling obituaries one way for one family, another way for another family. Families should be left with realistic expectations about what will be published. Many feel that they should control the content of an obituary, but the newspaper cannot allow this.

An obituary in The Washington Post is a news story, a straightforward summary of the principal events of a life. Like other news stories, obituaries should reflect the world as it is, rather than as we or the families of the deceased might wish it to be, and they should answer the usual questions: who, what, where, when and why.

That means obituaries, as news stories, should include such information as the age of the deceased and the medical cause of death or the circumstances that led to it. Painful details cannot be omitted simply because they are painful. But death is the enemy of common sense and special care must be taken to ensure that common sense prevails and yet no one is offended. It is sometimes helpful to explain to families that we require certain information about a death simply because obituaries are part of the news report, which means that they are entirely our responsibility and we write and edit them ourselves, as we do with all news stories. This is not widely understood.

Here are the policies that govern the publication of obituaries in The Washington Post.

General

An obituary is a straightforward account of the principal events of a life, including age and the medical cause of death. It is not a eulogy. We make no mention of funeral services, visiting, interment or expressions of sympathy.

We are prepared to write about any private person who has lived in the Washington area in a permanent way, even if he or she lived elsewhere at the time of death. We also publish brief obituaries about children of residents of the Washington area. The standard that determines whose obituary is published is residence, rather than rank or accomplishment.

In addition to age and cause of death, required information includes details of the person's career, education where it is relevant (for example, lawyers must have gone to law school), place of residence, religious or other affiliations if any, and the family, including previous spouses. (The deceased's exact address will not be published. Only the community of residence will be given in the newspaper.) If for any reason a family decides not to give us this information, no obituary will be published.

There is no set definition of how long a person has to live in the Washington area for the newspaper to publish an obituary. In general, military officers and government officials whose few years' tenure here was incidental to full lives elsewhere are excluded. Exceptions are made for topical reasons that are readily apparent, such as Medal of Honor winners or other distinctions.

Timing

Whenever possible, an obituary will be published the day after we receive the required information. If it is not possible, the obituary will be published the day after that. This should always be explained to the family. We do not do an obituary more than two weeks after death.

Except in the case of an inherently newsworthy individual whose obituary must be published in the next morning's newspaper, the lead of an obituary should use the date of death, rather than yesterday.

> *John Black, a retired English teacher in the Prince George's County public schools, died Nov. 8 in Panama City, Fla.*

Death Notices

Death notices, the boxed, alphabetized listings on the obituary page, are classified advertisements. They usually announce a death and list details of services and interment. The death notices are the only place where such information is published. Except for questions of libel and taste, the rules about news obituaries do not apply to death notices. People who buy space for such a notice have control over what it says and when it appears—the control they do not have over a news obituary. Death notices are handled by the classified advertising department.

Cause of Death

The medical cause of death is often a source of confusion. We do not use *long illness, short illness, heart failure, old age* etc. These are not medical terms. What caused the heart to fail? It could have been anything from a gunshot wound to Alzheimer's disease to a myocardial infarction, or heart attack.

Many families do not know the cause of death or even that a medical cause of death will have been determined ("She was 96.

What else could it be but old age?"). The easiest thing is to suggest
they call the funeral home, find out what was on the death certificate
and call us back.

Having found the cause of death, we try to explain it so that
the reader can understand it. If the death certificate says, for example,
"arteriosclerotic cardiovascular disease," the obituary will say a heart
ailment—not heart failure.

In the case of AIDS the obituary will say that the person "had
AIDS," not that he or she died of AIDS. AIDS itself does not cause
death.

In cases of violent or accidental death, we always consult the
police or the medical examiner and use their version of the circumstances. We always include the fact of suicide or homicide. It is not
possible to give a straightforward summary of a life that ends in
suicide without mentioning the suicide.

Family and Survivors

The list of survivors and the family makeup is often a sensitive
matter. We list spouses, children, siblings if any and surviving
parents by name and by town of residence. We report the number
of surviving grandchildren and great-grandchildren, if any, but not
their names or towns of residence. We do not list cousins, nieces,
nephews, aunts or uncles, or in-laws.

We also will list a longtime companion in either a heterosexual
or homosexual relationship. If the family of the deceased takes a
death notice that includes the companion as a survivor, or if we
have other reliable knowledge of the relationship, we will include
it in a news obituary in the same place where we would list a wife
or husband. The formula is:

Survivors include his longtime companion, John Doe, etc.

The obituary always accounts for marriages because a marriage is an important event in any life. While in general we do not list relatives of the first degree such as siblings who have died earlier, we always account for husbands and wives, whether the husband or wife survives and whether the marriage ended in death or divorce. This not only completes the summary of a life's events, it removes from our stories such anomalies as a Mary Smith leaving a son named John Jones. The reader could guess how that happened, but explaining it eliminates the need for guessing. A useful formula is:

Her marriage to Edward Jones ended in divorce

or

Her first husband, Edward Jones, died in 1962. Survivors include her husband, Bill Smith, of Wheaton; a son by her first marriage, John Jones, of Annandale; two children by her second marriage, etc.

Confirming Death

It is an inflexible rule that any death must be confirmed by an independent source before an obituary is published. The easiest way to do this is through the funeral home. Obituary writers should not accept the telephone number of a funeral home from the person giving the obituary information. To avoid the possibility of a hoax, the number of the funeral home should be looked up in the telephone directory.

Checking the Library

We check the news library for a file on everyone we write about. Occasionally these checks turn up some information the family did not wish to supply, such as a criminal conviction. Where a conviction or other disreputable act comes to light, the family should be advised that it will be included in the obituary. As with other information, such as previous marriages, this requirement may result in a request from the family that the obituary be withdrawn. In the case of a private individual the paper will be guided by the family's wishes.

Photographs

The Washington Post is asked to use a great many photographs. For reasons of space we can use very few. This should be explained to callers. When space permits, we will consider recent photographs—that is, recent enough to be a reasonable likeness of the deceased. Any photograph, color or black and white, taken by whatever process, can be copied in a few minutes and returned to the bearer. An old photograph may be used when there is a topical reason for doing so, such as the admiral in uniform as he retired in 1967.

Titles and Honorifics

Unlike the rest of the newspaper, obituaries use honorifics. John Smith is Mr. Smith on second reference. Mary Brown is Mrs. Brown, Miss Brown or Ms. Brown, depending on the family's preference. The title *Dr.* is used for anyone who held it, whether the doctorate was in medicine or some other field, earned or honorary. Military ranks are used when appropriate. It is not necessary to say, for example, *retired Air Force colonel John Smith* because the text of the obituary will make clear that he was retired and had been in the Air Force. Use *Col. John Smith*.

CHAPTER 5

USING THE LANGUAGE

This chapter is to be used as a guide to Washington Post style and preference on matters of spelling, punctuation, usage, numeration, capitalization, terminology, taste and policy on sensitive verbal issues. Items are listed alphabetically. An entry standing alone, without an explanation, such as *Hanukah* and *rock-and-roll*, indicates Washington Post spelling preference. Exceptions to Webster's New World Dictionary, third edition, are marked with an asterisk. Examples are in *italics*. Cross-references are in SMALL CAPITALS.

a, an
Sound, not spelling, determines which is used. The indefinite article *a* is used with words that begin with a sounded *h*: *a historic day, a hotel in London.* The word *an* is used before words beginning with an unsounded *h*: *an honor, an heir.* A also is used before words beginning with vowels that are sounded like consonants: *a union, a Eucharist service.*

abbreviations

In general, abbreviations are used to save space and aid comprehension. Abbreviation style is more flexible in headlines, graphics and tabular matter than in text. (Throughout this stylebook, what is permissible in headlines is also understood to be permissible in graphics and in tabular matter.)

Some abbreviations and acronyms are so well known that they are part of the language and may be used on first reference without elaboration: *DDT, IOU, FBI, CIA, NAACP, AIDS, PCP, LSD, TNT* (See 3a, below). Some are well known in specific subject areas and may be used on first reference in sections devoted to those subjects—especially sports—but should be spelled out on first reference in other sections: *NBA* in the Sports section, *National Basketball Association* elsewhere. Some abbreviations are appropriate only in headlines in certain sections: *NSO* for National Symphony Orchestra in the Style section, *LBO* for leveraged buyout in the Business section. These are judgment calls for editors, and each section's list will change over time.

All-capitals abbreviations other than place names generally do not take periods: *CBS, NAACP, EST, GOP, OPEC, GNP.* Other abbreviations generally do take periods: *U.N., N.Y., U.S.S.R., c.o.d., Ave., Sgt.*

In general, abbreviations other than *Dr.* are not used in quotations of spoken matter. See QUOTATIONS. For abbreviations not dealt with in this heading, see ACRONYMS; MUSIC; TITLES; MILITARY RANKS AND TITLES; NUMERALS.

1. **Measurement and time**
   a. Common abbreviations of technical measurement are lowercase without periods when used with specific numbers: *55 mph, 3,000 rpm.* Omit the space before millimeter and kilobyte: *a 105mm howitzer, 256k of memory.* Terms that are less familiar should be spelled out in first reference,

followed by the abbreviation in parentheses if it will recur in the story. If it will not recur, omit the abbreviation: *20 British thermal units (Btu), 40 kilohertz (kHz), 30 pounds per square inch (psi).* In text, such terms as *year, hour, mile, meter, pound, cent* etc. are spelled out. They may be abbreviated in headlines and tabular matter. In recipes, units of measurement are spelled out and quantities are given in numerals: *3 ounces, ¼ cup, 2 tablespoons.*

b. Do not abbreviate *March, April, May, June* or *July.* The other months are abbreviated in specific dates: *Dec. 7, 1941. Your paper is due Nov. 30.*

c. Use *A.D.* and *B.C.* but *a.m.* and *p.m.* Use *EST, PDT* etc. See TIME.

2. **Places**

a. Spell out *United States* as a noun. Use the abbreviation *U.S.* as an adjective and in headlines and captions. Use *U.S.A.* in direct quotation only. See also UNITED STATES. Do not use periods when the initials are part of the name of an organization, ship etc.: *USIA, USS Kitty Hawk.*

b. Do not abbreviate names of U.S. possessions, foreign nations or Canadian provinces other than *B.C.* (British Columbia), except when necessary to save space in headlines: *He was born in Saskatoon, Saskatchewan. They came from Santurce, Puerto Rico. His home is in Pretoria, South Africa.* A headline such as *Angola Rejects S. Africa Plan* or *Soviet Warns W. Germany* is unsightly but sometimes necessary.

c. Do not abbreviate *Alaska, Hawaii, Idaho, Iowa, Maine, Ohio* or *Utah.* The names of other states are abbreviated in addresses and after the names of towns, cities, counties and physical locations such as a national park or military base. Use the standard abbreviations (not the Postal Ser-

vice's two-letter abbreviations): *Ala.*, *Ariz.*, *Ark.*, *Calif.*,
Colo., *Conn.*, *D.C.*, *Del.*, *Fla.*, *Ga.*, *Ill.*, *Ind.*, *Kan.*, *Ky.*,
La., *Mass.*, *Md.*, *Mich.*, *Minn.*, *Miss.*, *Mo.*, *Mont.*, *N.C.*,
N.D., *Neb.*, *Nev.*, *N.H.*, *N.J.*, *N.M.*, *N.Y.*, *Okla*, *Ore.*,
Pa., *R.I.*, *S.C.*, *S.D.*, *Tenn.*, *Tex.*, *Va.*, *Vt.*, *Wash.*, *Wis.*,
W. Va., *Wyo.*

d. In text, do not abbreviate the names of cities or counties
or of places such as *Long Island*. Spell out *District of Columbia*, *the District*, as a noun. *D.C.* may be used as an
adjective.

e. All-capitals abbreviations such as *D.C.*, *N.Y.*, *L.A.* and
P.G. (for Prince George's County) may be used in head-
lines. Do not use P.W. for Prince William County or
A.A. for Anne Arundel County.

f. Abbreviate specific addresses but spell out general loca-
tions: *She lived at 2390 P St. NW; The store is at 11978
Crain Hwy. The accident occurred at 23rd and P streets NW.
They drove south on Route 15.* See also ADDRESSES.

g. Do not abbreviate *Lane*, *Oval*, *Plaza*, *Route*, *Pike*, *Point* or
Port.

h. Do not abbreviate *Fort* or *Mount* except to save space in
headlines. *Saint* is abbreviated in places and the names of
churches and institutions, spelled out in the names of
canonized individuals: *St. Paul, Minn.; St. Paul's Church;
the epistles of Saint Paul; St. Elizabeths Hospital.* Exception:
Saint John, New Brunswick.

3. Organizations

The use of an organization's initials depends on how recog-
nizable they are. The list of organizations of which the initials
are so familiar that they can stand alone varies from time to

time and from context to context. There is no firm list of organizations in this category. A good test is whether the initials are better known or more widely recognized than the full name of the organization or institution.

a. The list of initials that are so well known that the name need not be spelled out unless desired for emphasis includes, but is not necessarily limited to: *ABC, AFL-CIO, BBC, CARE, CBS, CIA, FBI, GOP, NAACP, NATO, NBC, NCAA, PTA, ROTC, UCLA, U.N., UNESCO, UNICEF*. Corporate names are spelled out on first reference no matter how well known they are unless the abbreviation has been adopted as the formal corporate name: *International Business Machines Corp.; USF & G Corp*. See CORPORATE NAMES.

b. Less familiar initials may be used in headlines and text but the full name should be spelled out at some point close to the first reference, preferably before the initials are used. Among the organizations in this category are *NASA*, the *PLO*, the *IRA, TVA, GATT* and *OPEC*. *He worked for the National Aeronautics and Space Administration. NASA was then preparing to launch its first orbiter. She foresaw the impact of the Tennessee Valley Authority before TVA built its first dam. The negotiations will be within the framework of the General Agreement on Tariffs and Trade, but no one believes GATT procedures can produce an agreement. The outlawed Irish Republican Army disavowed the killing, the first time the IRA has issued such a statement. Oil ministers from six OPEC nations agreed yesterday on production cutbacks to bolster crude oil prices. But it was unclear whether the agreement would be approved by the full membership of the Organization of Petroleum Exporting Countries*. See also ACRONYMS.

c. The initials of little-known and ad hoc organizations should be used only to avoid excessive repetition of the full name.

On first reference, spell out the name and enclose the initials in parentheses. *They were opposed by an unusual alliance of the National Retail Dry Goods Association (NRDGA) and a citizens group called Justice for Migrant Labor (JML).*

d. For simplicity's sake, lengthy but familiar names may be abbreviated on first reference but spelled out at the first opportunity: *The only member of Reagan's Cabinet who served the full eight years was HUD Secretary Samuel Pierce. Pierce, who led the Housing and Urban Development Department through difficult times. . . .*

e. Spell out *United Nations* as a noun. Use the abbreviation *U.N.*, with periods, in headlines and as an adjective. Omit periods in all-capitals abbreviations of U.N. organizations: *UNESCO, UNICEF, UNCTAD.*

f. Use the abbreviations *Co., Corp., Inc., Bros.* etc. in corporate names but spell out the words in cultural and military usage: *R.H. Macy & Co., the Metropolitan Opera Company, Charlie Company, Engine Company 12.*

g. Generally avoid government and military jargon abbreviations such as *DOE* and *CINCPAC.* Where they must be used, as in quotations, spell them out between parentheses or brackets. The initials of a few federal government departments—*USDA, OMB, DOT, HHS*—may be familiar to Washington readers and may be used sparingly as nouns or adjectives, but not on first reference: *Inspectors from the Agriculture Department seized the entire shipment. They said it had not been inspected according to USDA regulations.*

h. In text, spell out *association, bureau, department* and *division.* In headlines, *Department* may be abbreviated as *Dept.*

i. Do not abbreviate *attorney general, auditor general, comman-*

dant, detective, district attorney, governor general, secretary, secretary general or superintendent. See also GOVERNOR.

4. **Miscellaneous**
   a. Academic degrees and religious orders are abbreviated without periods: *LLD, MA, BS, PhD, DD, MD, SJ.*

   b. The names of colleges and universities may be abbreviated or given in initial form if the abbreviation or initials are familiar: *UCLA, SMU, MIT.* Avoid initials where they could apply to more than one school. *OSU* could mean Ohio State, Oklahoma State or Oregon State. The names of *American, Georgetown, George Washington, Howard, George Mason* and *Catholic* universities, the *University of the District of Columbia*, the *University of Virginia* and the *University of Maryland* are spelled out except in headlines. In headlines, all but *Howard* may be abbreviated: *AU, CU, GU, GWU, GMU, UDC, U-Va., U-Md.*

   c. Abbreviate the word *number* and use figures in the serial sense only—that is, where an actual numbered list exists: *He was the No. 1 draft choice; ranked No. 5 in the country. She'll never be higher than number four or five in this company. He said it was his number one priority.* Abbreviate, capitalize and use the numeral in headlines and when referring to a specific numbered list: *The Redskins' No. 1 draft choice.* Do not abbreviate *number* in direct quotation: *"We're number one," the students chanted.* Do not abbreviate other serial terms: *Chapter 3, Figure 6.* See also NUMERALS.

   d. Abbreviate political and state designations of legislators: *Rep. John Black (R-Tenn.), Sen. Mary White (D-Vt.).* In stories that deal entirely with one type of legislator or members of one party, do not use these parenthetical designations to repeat information given in the text: *At the*

Republican National Convention, three representatives from Texas held the spotlight: John Black, Mary White and George Smith—not *Rep. John Black (R-Tex.)* etc. The reader already knows Black is a Republican representative from Texas. *On the Senate side, the Democratic conferees were John Green (N.Y.), Mary White (Vt.) and George Smith (Mont.)*—not *Sen. John Green (D-N.Y.)* etc. The reader has already been told that Green is a senator and a Democrat.

e. Do not abbreviate or capitalize nonmilitary titles after *former, retired* or *the late.* See FORMER, RETIRED.

f. Do not abbreviate books of the Bible.

g. On first reference, do not abbreviate vernacular abbreviations outside the context of the section of the paper where they normally appear: *RBI* in sports stories, *runs batted in* elsewhere; *LBOs* in business stories, *leveraged buyouts* elsewhere.

h. Generally avoid abbreviations in direct quotations of speech. See QUOTATIONS.

abortion
See RIGHT-TO-LIFE.

academic
As a noun, academic means a scholar, usually on the faculty of a university. Academician means a member of a particular academy: *His research was scorned by academics. Members of the French Academy treat other academicians scornfully.*

academic degrees
See ABBREVIATIONS.

accent marks

a. For English words—i.e., those that are not italicized in Webster's New World Dictionary and not italicized in the newspaper—accent marks and diacritical marks such as the tilde are omitted except:

   i. where the accent mark is necessary to avoid ambiguity, as in *à la*. *She wore a pillbox hat, à la Jackie Kennedy.*

   ii. where there exists another word that is spelled the same way and only the accent marks differentiate between them. Words considered by the dictionary to be English words such as *facade, decor, detente, chateau* and *soupcon* do not need the marks because there are no other words that could be confused with them. But accent marks are used when necessary to distinguish an English word from another with the same spelling: *résumé* as distinct from *resume*; *pâté* as distinct from *pate*.

b. Foreign words, the words italicized in the dictionary or otherwise not part of the English language, should not be used when there is an English equivalent or easy translation: *turn of the century*, not *fin de siècle*; *established case law*, not *stare decisis*. Where a foreign word must be used, use the accents and diacritical marks in French and Spanish words, which are most familiar to readers and most accessible to editors: *el niño; à bas les prêtres*. Omit them in words from other languages. The German vowel-and-umlaut appears as vowel-and-e: *Guenther Grass.*

c. Foreign place names and the names of individuals do not require accent marks: *Andre Malraux; the Gaspe Peninsula; Jorge Luis Gomez.* See also GEOGRAPHIC NAMES.

d. Accents and diacritical marks are omitted in headlines and graphics.

Achilles' heel, Achilles' tendon

acronyms

An acronym is a commonly understood word made up of the initials of other words: *AIDS* (acquired immune deficiency syndrome) and *scuba* (self-contained underwater breathing apparatus) are acronyms. So is *Geico*, originally Government Employees Insurance Co. Mere abbreviations are not acronyms, however much they may be part of everyday language: FBI, IBM, PLO, CIA, NBA, CBS etc. are not acronyms.

Nowadays it's common for publicity-conscious ad hoc groups to pick an acronym that supports their cause, such as FAIR or BRAVE, and adopt a name to go with the initials. Try to avoid acronyms that make such editorial statements. Use *the community organization* or *the citizens group*.

a. Acronyms are capitalized unless they have become words in their own right: *DEW line* (for distant early warning); *GATT* (for General Agreement on Tariffs and Trade); *RICO,* (the Racketeer Influenced and Corrupt Organizations Act); *scuba* (self-contained underwater breathing apparatus); *laser* (light amplification by stimulated emission of radiation). One exception is *AIDS*, which has become a word in its own right but is capitalized to avoid confusion with an existing word. Another exception is *WASP*. Follow the style in Webster's New World Dictionary. See also COM-PUTER LANGUAGE.

b. In corporate acronyms, capitalize the first letter only, regardless of the preference of the corporation: *Geico, Pepco, Alcoa*.

act, bill, law

Proposed legislation is a bill. After legislative approval and signature by the executive, it becomes an act, and its provisions become a law. In describing the provisions of a bill, use *would prohibit*, not *will prohibit*. The names of acts are capitalized: *Foreign Corrupt Practices Act, Employee Retirement Income Security Act*. Bills are lowercase except when their formal title is used. Note that the formal title of a bill usually contains the word act even if the bill has little chance of passage: *The Electric Power Consumers' Protection Act of 1988*. These formal titles should be used with caution because they often obscure the real purpose of a bill. See also CAPITALIZATION, 2.

Adams-Morgan

Hyphenate the neighborhood in Northwest Washington.

addresses

Complete street addresses are used only when the precise location is essential to the story: *The fire destroyed the house at 2187 Elm St. and threatened the houses on both sides of it. The tenants began a rent strike because they said their building, at 5298 Connecticut Ave. NW, was unfit to live in.*

In crime stories especially and in any other stories in which publication of a precise address could bring harm, embarrassment or harassment to an innocent person, use block numbers rather than exact addresses: *The shooting took place in the 1100 block of Rockville Pike. Police arrested Ann Johnson, of the 3300 block of East Capitol Street, and George Williams, of the unit block of 48th Street NE*. Do not give the exact address of a living crime or accident victim. In obituaries, give the town or community only: *She lived in Laurel. He lived in Falls Church*. For style on building numbers and numbered streets, see NUMERALS. For style on abbreviation of words such as road, avenue and boulevard, see ABBREVIATIONS. See also EAST CAPITOL STREET.

adopted, adoptive

Do not use *adoptive* or *adopted* unless the information is clearly pertinent to the story—when the legality of the adoption is in question, for example, or in an incest case. When John and Mary Smith adopt a child, he or she becomes their child, no different from any other. Adoptive parents and adopted children are offended when an unnecessary distinction is drawn between them and other families.

adrenaline*
Adrenalin is a trade name.

adverse, averse
Adverse means unfavorable. *Averse to* means opposed. *They worked in adverse conditions. He was averse to working late.*

adviser*

Advisory Neighborhood Commission
Abbreviated *ANC* in headlines and on second reference.

affect, effect
Affect is a verb meaning to influence, to have an effect on. *Effect*, as a verb, means to bring about. As a noun, it means result. *His short punt didn't affect the outcome of the game. She was unable to effect any change in the system. Her efforts had no effect.*

AFL-CIO
The abbreviation may be used in all references to the American Federation of Labor and Congress of Industrial Organizations.

age
A person's age is generally given after the name unless it is to be emphasized: *John Smith, 35; the 103-year-old John Smith.* When age is relevant to a story it may be discussed, but beware of adjectives such as *elderly, middle-aged* etc. Young reporters especially tend to use these words about people who would not appreciate them. See also JUVENILES and PHYSICAL APPEARANCE.

aggravate

The word *aggravate* means to make worse. Do not use as a synonym for irritate or annoy. *The hospital bill aggravated the distress caused by his illness.*

aid, aide

To *aid* is to assist. An *aide* is an assistant. The word *aide* is so vague that it should be reserved for headlines and avoided in text. Try to specify the position or role of the person involved.

AIDS

    a. The acronym for acquired immune deficiency syndrome may stand alone, without elaboration, on all references. See ACRONYMS.

    b. AIDS is a sensitive subject. In general, use *AIDS patient*, not *AIDS victim*. AIDS itself does not kill but it allows other diseases to kill. In obituaries and other stories involving AIDS deaths, say: *He had AIDS*, not *He died of AIDS*.

air base, Air Force base

Follow the style of the U.S. Air Force, which uses air force base in the United States, air base abroad: *Andrews Air Force Base; Clark Air Base, the Philippines.* Do not abbreviate, except *AFB* in headlines. Capitalize in the names of specific installations: *A Canadian air base; Andrews Air Force Base; an Air Force base in North Dakota.*

aircraft

The names of civilian and military aircraft are hyphenated when the hyphen appears in the manufacturer's nomenclature or official military designation: *L-1011, F-15; Boeing 747B.* Missiles and space launchers take Roman numerals: *Pershing II, Minuteman III.* Spell out *Air Force One*, the president's plane. Consult Jane's All the World's Aircraft. See also WEAPONS AND WEAPONS SYSTEMS.

airline

Airline is one word except in the name of an airline company or organization that uses two words: *American Airlines, Japan Air Lines, Air Line Pilots Association.* The names of major airlines can be checked in the telephone directory. Note, however, that Eastern Airlines is owned by Eastern Air Lines Inc. Use *Eastern Airlines* to refer to the carrier and its operations, *Eastern Air Lines* to refer to the corporation, as in articles about its sale.

airport

Capitalize when it is part of a formal or official name: *National Airport; La Guardia Airport. Its name is Bradley International Airport.* Lowercase as a generic term: *He landed at the Hartford airport.*

Alger, Horatio

Horatio Alger (1832–1899) was a prolific writer of books about young men who rose from poverty to success, mostly through clean living, hard work and good luck. That is, Alger was the author of the books, not their hero. Alger did not rise from poverty or pull himself up by his bootstraps. He grew up middle-class and went to Harvard. Beware of such phrases as *a hero in the mold of Horatio Alger.*

all ready (prepared); already (previously)
She's all ready to go. They have already left.

all right; never alright

all together (grouped); altogether (in total, thoroughly)
They were all together in Paris. There were 11 altogether.

all-American (noun); *all-America* (adjective)
He was an all-American at Clemson. He was an all-America basketball player.

Allegany County (Md.); *Alleghany* County (Va.); *Allegheny* County (Pa.); *Allegheny* River; *Allegheny* Mountains

allegedly

This word is used to indicate that the newspaper is reporting a charge or accusation made by someone else, a charge the newspaper does not necessarily believe: *Jones allegedly embezzled $2 million.* The word should be omitted when the sentence specifies that the police or some other legal authority is making the allegation. *Police said he stole a car.* (Not *Police said he allegedly stole a car*, which is incorrect. The police didn't say that.) *The indictment charged that she embezzled $2 million.* (Not *The indictment charged that she allegedly embezzled $2 million.*) Note that the use of this disclaimer word does not protect the paper from the consequences of publishing libelous material. See Chapter 2.

all-star

Capitalize in references to a specific game. *He played in the National Hockey League All-Star Game in Montreal.*

allusion, illusion

An *allusion* is an indirect reference. An *illusion* is a false impression. Something or someone that is identified is referred to, not alluded to. *His joke about Hoosiers was an allusion to Vice President Quayle. He had the illusion that he would be taken seriously as a writer.*

ambiance*

America, Americans
See UNITED STATES.

Americas Cup (golf); America's Cup (sailing)

amok, not amuck

ampersand
The ampersand (&) is used when it is part of the formal title of a company or organization: *Ferris & Co.; Newport News Shipbuilding & Dry Dock Co.; U.S. News & World Report; Hogan & Hartson* (and most other law firms). It is also used in abbreviations consisting entirely of capital letters: *AT & T, B & O Railroad.* It is not otherwise used in place of *and* except when necessary in feature headlines.

angst*

anti-
See PREFIXES.

any more,* anymore
Two words except as an adverb expressing time in negative sentences: *Do you want any more soup? We never go there anymore.*

any one, anyone
Any one means any single person or thing: *He didn't name any one country as the aggressor. Anyone* means any person at all. *She didn't hurt anyone.*

apostrophe
The apostrophe is used to indicate omissions and contractions and to form possessives of nouns: *John's dog won't hunt.* It is also used to form the plurals of single letters.

1. **Omissions**
   a. Do not use an apostrophe to indicate a shortened form of a word if the short form is listed as a primary spelling in *Webster's New World*: *copter*, not *'copter; gator*, not *'gator; Halloween; highfalutin.*

   b. Use an apostrophe, sparingly, to indicate omissions in quoted colloquial speech and in poetic usage: *I've got 'em now. Y'all come. O'er the fields.*

   c. Use an apostrophe to indicate omitted numbers: *class of '47; she was born in the '50s.* But *the 1988–89 season.*

2. **Possessives**
   a. Use *'s* to indicate possession after nouns not ending in *s*: *Lopez's, dog's, prince's, children's, Ford Motor Co.'s, box's, Marx's, B-52's* (as a possessive, not as a plural). Exceptions: *Red Sox', White Sox'.*

   b. Use *'s* to form the possessive of singular nouns, proper names and nicknames ending in a sounded *s*: *Lucas's new movie, the boss's secretary, the Boss's big concert, the chorus's big moment, the lass's skirt, Philip Glass's opera, Mars's anger, Zeus's wife, James's book, Dr. Seuss's books.* But use the apostrophe alone for proper names of more than one syllable ending in *-es*: *Demosthenes' orations, Xerxes' conquests.*

   c. Use the apostrophe alone to form the possessive of words ending in a silent *s*: *Arkansas' rice crop, Dubois' Free Quebec campaign, the Marine Corps' training program.*

   d. Plural possessives take the apostrophe only: *The Joneses' dog, the Williamses' car, the horses' feed, the princesses' jewels, the boys' football.*

   e. Do not use the apostrophe in possessive pronouns: *His, its, hers, theirs* etc.

f. When the possessive applies to more than one person, use a single apostrophe to show common possession, separate apostrophes to show separate possession: *John and Mary's house; John's and Mary's clothes.*

g. Use an apostrophe in certain idiomatic phrases that take the possessive form even though there is no actual ownership: *a day's wages, for old times' sake, two hours' travel, a friend of Bill's,* but *two days overdue, eight months pregnant.*

h. Use an apostrophe in a proper noun when it is part of the official name: *Actors Equity, Prince George's County, the San Francisco 49ers, New Year's Day, Pikes Peak.* Many names are listed in this stylebook and in the dictionary.

3. **Plurals**

The apostrophe is used to form a plural only for the plurals of single letters, whether capital or lowercase: *He got straight A's. Be sure to cross all your i's and dot all your t's.* The apostrophe is not used for any other plurals: *the 1960s, the '60s; he shot in the low 80s; no ifs, ands or buts; thises and thats.* Exception: *do's and don'ts.*

appraise, apprise

Appraise is to set a monetary value on; *apprise* means to inform.

Arabic words and names

The transliteration of Arabic words and names into English always presents difficulties. There is no single approved system, as there is with Chinese. Some Arabic names are commonly transliterated in French spellings: *Camille Chamoun*, not *Kamil Shamun*. Others are known by the anglicized transliteration, not the French: *Anwar Sadat*, not *Anouar el-Sadate*. Even individual letters are transliterated differently: the Arabic *qaf* is sometimes *q* (*Sultan Qaboos* of Oman), sometimes *k* (*Farouk Kaddoumi* of the PLO, not *Farouq Qaddoumi*).

The names of many places and people in Arabic contain the definite article, transliterated el- or al- but sometimes elided into the succeeding consonant as an-, at-, ash- etc.: *an-Nahar* (newspaper), *at-Talia* (magazine).

a. In general, prominent Arab individuals and newsworthy institutions have their own preferred English spellings, which they will use in diplomatic lists, reports by official news agencies and English-language publications. Use these spellings except for the definite article: Thus *Mohamed Heikal*, not *Mohammed*; *Tewfik Hakim*, not *Tawfiq*.

b. The article is used, with hyphen, in names of organizations such as newspapers and in place names: *al-Ahram* (newspaper); *el-Alamein, Sharm el-Sheik* (places in Egypt); *al-Azhar University*. The hyphen is omitted when the article has been absorbed into the name: *Algiers, Alhambra*. See also GEOGRAPHIC NAMES. Generally omit the article and hyphen in names of individuals: *Hafez Assad, president of Syria*, not *Hafez al-Assad*. But use the article when the individual has dropped the hyphen and run the article together with the word: *Mohammed Alsheikh*.

c. Individual names: *Abdul* and *Abdel* (meaning servant of), *ibn* and *bin* (meaning son of) and *Abu* (meaning father of) are not names that stand by themselves or middle names. Thus the terrorist Abu Nidal is *Abu Nidal* on second reference, never *Nidal* alone. (Two prominent individuals were exceptions: *King Abdul-Aziz ibn Saud*, founder of Saudi Arabia, should be *Abdul-Aziz* on second reference, and in the Middle East that is how he is known, but in the West he is called *King Ibn Saud*. *Gamal Abdel Nasser* of Egypt is always *Abdel Nasser* on second reference in Arabic, but convention prevailed in English and he became *Nasser*.) *Abdul* or *Abdel* rarely stands alone as a given name. On second reference, Arabs use their family names unless they are royalty: *Hosni Mubarak* is *Mubarak, Ahmed Zaki Yamani* is *Yamani*, but *Qaboos ibn Said*, sultan of Oman, is *Qaboos; King Hussein ibn Talal* of Jordan is *Hussein*.

d. Many Arab men are named after the prophet Muhammad, founder of Islam, but spellings vary: *Mohammed, Muhammad, Mohamed.* When the individual's preference can be ascertained, as from an official news agency or the diplomatic list, it should be used. Otherwise, *Muhammad.*

e. The ruler of Libya is *Moammar Gadhafi.*

architect

An architect is a person who has passed the Architecture Registration Examination and met other licensing requirements in the state in which he or she practices. Membership in the American Institute of Architects is a professional option and has nothing to do with licensing. Not everyone who designs a room or even an entire building is an architect. Terms for nonlicensed architectural draftsmen include designer, residential designer and project designer.

Arlington County Board, the County Board, the board
See CAPITALIZATION, 3i.

army

Capitalize when referring to the U.S. Army and when the word is part of an official or formal designation in a foreign army: *People's Liberation Army, the British 8th Army.* Lowercase as a generic designation for the ground troops of other nations: *French army, Israeli army.* See CAPITALIZATION, 5b.

Army Reserve

Capitalize when referring to the specific organization: the *U.S. Army Reserve, the Army Reserve.* Lowercase *reserve* in general references: *The president activated the reserves.* Similarly, *the Naval Reserve, an Air Force Reserve squadron. Three reserve units use this armory.*

ascent, assent

An *ascent* is a climb. An *assent* is an agreement. The word that means the act of ascending is ascension, as in ascension to the throne.

Associated Press

In credit lines at the beginning of a story, without the article. Not *the Associated Press.* In text, *the Associated Press. The story was reported by the Associated Press.*

assure, ensure, insure

These three words, which have entirely different meanings, are often confused. To *assure* is to promise, to remove worry or uncertainty. To *ensure* is to make an outcome inevitable. To *insure* is to provide insurance. *I assure you that I can ensure that his company will insure your car.*

Atlantic Coast Conference

Abbreviated as *ACC*. The members are the universities of Maryland, Virginia and North Carolina, North Carolina State University, Duke, Clemson, Wake Forest and Georgia Tech. In sports stories only, the abbreviation is acceptable on first reference.

attorney general

Do not abbreviate. The plural is *attorneys general.*

attorney, lawyer

The words are not synonyms. The generic term for a person who holds a law degree is lawyer: *He came to court with his lawyer. She wants to become a lawyer.* An attorney is one who acts as agent for, or in behalf of, another person or organization: *She gave her son power of attorney.* An attorney is a lawyer only if he or she is an attorney at law. *Attorney who represents* is redundant; use *attorney for*. Many lawyers, such as those on the staffs of congressional committees, do not work as attorneys.

auger, augur
An *auger* is a tool for boring. *Augur*, a verb, means to be an omen of.

author
Do not use as a verb. The verb is *write*.

average, median
The words have different meanings. The distinction between them is important, especially in stories involving polls, demographics, test scores and the like.

   a. *Average*, or arithmetic mean, is the number obtained by dividing the sum of a set of numbers by the number of numbers in the set. To find the average of 5, 6, 10 and 15, first add them, then divide by 4, which is the number of numbers in the set. The average is 9.

   b. The *median* is the point at which half the numbers in a set are higher, half lower. The use of a median rather than average figure often gives a more accurate picture of a numerical situation because it eliminates the single anomalous number that distorts the average. If, for example, there are six people in a group and their ages are 3, 5, 7, 9, 12 and 84, their average age is 20, which makes it sound as if they are a group of young adults. But their median age is 8, which gives a more accurate picture.

average person
There is no average person. Avoid this expression.

awhile, a while
While is a noun meaning period of time. *Awhile* is an adverb meaning for a short time. *She asked him to stay awhile. She asked him to stay for a while. For awhile* is redundant.

ayatollah
The word literally means sign from God. It is a title awarded to the most senior teachers and judges in the Shiite branch of Islam, as practiced in Iran. An ayatollah is not a clergyman. There is no ordained clergy in Islam. Capitalize only as a title: *He was loyal to the ayatollah. He admired Ayatollah Khomeini.*

baby-sit, baby-sitting; babysitter*
Baby-sit is an intransitive verb: *He was baby-sitting for his 3-year-old niece.*

back seat (noun); back-seat (adj.); back talk, back yard
For other compounds beginning with *back-*, see COMPOUND WORDS.

ball, ball-
See COMPOUND WORDS. Follow the style of Webster's New World Dictionary: *ball bearing, ball boy; ballgame, ballhandler, ballpark.* Exception: *ballclub.**

baloney, bologna
Baloney is nonsense. The sliced luncheon meat is *bologna.*

Baltimore
The city is identified as Baltimore City when necessary to distinguish it from Baltimore County, a separate jurisdiction. *The governor met with the Baltimore City delegation.*

bankruptcy
All bankruptcy proceedings are conducted in U.S. Bankruptcy Court.

Always specify the chapter of the Federal Bankruptcy Act under which a case is filed: Chapter 11 (voluntary reorganization), Chapter 7 (liquidation) etc. A company that seeks court protection from its creditors under Chapter 11 should not be described as *bankrupt* or *filing for bankruptcy*—it may turn out to be solvent when it gets its affairs in order. Say *The XYZ Corp. has filed for protection from its creditors in Bankruptcy Court* or *The XYZ Corp. is in bankruptcy proceedings*, which means the court must approve all its financial transactions.

bar mitzvah (boys); **bat mitzvah** (girls)
Do not use as a verb.

*Beaux-Arts**
Use as an adjective only.

bemused
It means confused, not amused.

bestseller, best-selling

biannual, biennial
Biannual means semiannual, happening twice a year. For clarity, use *semiannual*. *Biennial* means every two years.

bible, biblical references
Bible is capitalized when referring to the scriptures of the Old and New testaments, otherwise not. *He swore on the Bible. The Daily Racing Form was his bible.* Citations from the Old and New testaments use this form: *Isaiah 2:17, Luke 19:1–13, 2 Timothy 1:1–10.* Do not abbreviate books of the Bible.

black-and-white

Hyphenate in reference to films and television. Omit hyphens in references to the two as colors. *Snow and darkness turned the landscape black and white. The movie they watched was in black-and-white.*

blizzard

Not every snowstorm is a blizzard. The National Weather Service says a blizzard is a storm with wind speeds of 35 mph or more, considerable falling and drifting snow and visibility near zero. Note that the depth of the snow is not part of the definition.

blond, blonde

Use *blond* as an adjective, or as a noun referring to a man. *Blonde* is used only as a noun referring to a woman and only when a reference to appearance is appropriate. *Her career took off after she became a blonde.* See also PHYSICAL APPEARANCE.

boat, ship

On second reference, use the pronoun *it*, not *she*.

borscht

bouillon, bullion

Bouillon is soup. *Bullion* is gold or silver in ingots.

brackets

See PARENTHESES AND BRACKETS and QUOTATIONS.

Brahman, Brahmin

Brahman is a Hindu caste or a breed of cattle. A *Brahmin* is a cultured, upper-class person, usually from New England. The term should be used with care.

brand names
See TRADE NAMES AND BRANDS.

breaststroke*

Broadway, off-Broadway, off-off-Broadway
In references to stage productions, these terms are distinctions made in labor contracts. They do not refer to the location of the theater. *Broadway* productions are in large theaters, usually with 300 or more seats, and have union pay scales. *Off-Broadway* means smaller houses and a lower pay scale. *Off-off-Broadway* means workshop and experimental productions in which union members may appear for a limited time or at substandard pay. *Broadway* may be used as a generic word for the New York theater district. *She set her sights on Broadway.*

Brooklyn
See DATELINES.

Burning Tree Club (not Country Club)

bylines
Reporters, editors and editorial aides employed by The Washington Post will be credited as *Washington Post Staff Writer* or *Washington Post Foreign Service* with their bylines. The contributions of all other employees, stringers and freelancers will carry the credit line *Special to The Washington Post*.

cabinet
The word is capitalized in references to the executive branch of the U.S. government or a state government: *President Bush met with members of his Cabinet. Congress resisted every one of his Cabinet appointments.* Lowercase in references to foreign governments: *Italian Prime Minister Amintore Fanfani reshuffled his cabinet.* Individual departments

of the U.S. government are capitalized in references to the department, lowercase as part of a title standing alone. *She transferred back and forth between Commerce and Labor but she never became secretary of labor.*

Caesarean section

caliber
See FIREARMS.

callous, callus
Callous is an adjective that means unfeeling. A *callus* (noun) is a patch of hardened skin.

cancel, postpone
To *cancel* is to do away with or wipe out. To *postpone* is to put off and reschedule. *The game was postponed because of bad weather* means it will be played in the future. *The game was canceled because of bad weather* means it will not be played.

capital, capitol

a. A *capital* is a city that is a seat of government. A *capitol* is the building where a legislature meets. *The U.S. Capitol; Oklahoma City is the state capital, site of the state Capitol.*

b. Note that different organizations and places in the Washington area use different spellings: *the Capital Hilton, Capitol Heights, the Capitol City Inn.* See also EAST CAPITOL STREET.

Capital Beltway, the Beltway
On road signs and highway maps, the eastern semicircle of the Capital Beltway is designated Interstate 95; the western semicircle

is I-495. To avoid confusion in news stories the I-95 designation should generally be reserved for the north-south portions of I-95 outside the Beltway: *The accident occurred on I-95 near Quantico; on I-95 north of Laurel; the accident occurred on the Beltway near Capital Centre; on the inner loop of the Beltway near the Mormon Temple.* The lanes of the Beltway on which traffic moves clockwise are the inner loop; those on which it moves counterclockwise are the outer loop.

Capital Centre

The name does not take a definite article: *The game was played at Capital Centre.*

capitalization

In general, names, proper nouns and adjectives, and official titles preceding names are capitalized in text.

In headlines, capitalize each word that begins a line and all other words except *a, an, the, or, if, by, to, of, and, but, off, on, in, as, at* and *for.* These are lowercase except when part of a verb phrase, at the beginning of a line or as the last word in a headline. *Suspect Says He Had Nothing to Live For. A Fan's Advice for Players: Stop Goofing Off. Police Burst In on Gangsters.* The same words are generally lowercase in book and movie titles etc., except at the beginning: *"Going in Style," "Judd for the Defense," "In Harm's Way."*

For capitalization style of words not listed in this stylebook, consult Webster's New World Dictionary. See also TITLES; TRADE NAMES AND BRANDS; RELIGION AND THE CLERGY; FRATERNAL ORGANIZATIONS; TREES AND PLANTS; GEOGRAPHIC NAMES; MUSIC.

1. **Arts and letters**
   a. Capitalize the principal words in titles of books, paintings, plays, sculpture, songs and television programs: *Neil Sheehan's "A Bright Shining Lie," Michelangelo's "David," "ABC Monday Night Football," "60 Minutes."*

b. For artistic and literary styles and movements, follow the style of Webster's New World Dictionary: *impressionism, baroque, cubist, pointillism, dada, romanticism, rococo. Romanesque, Bauhaus, Gothic, Renaissance, Edwardian.* Exceptions: *Beaux-Arts** (which is used as an adjective only), *Federal** (the architectural period, not the adjective as in *federal court*).

c. Capitalize names of newspapers and periodicals, but lowercase *the* except in The Washington Post, The Post. It's *the New York Times Magazine, Le Monde, the Fairfax Journal.* Capitalize names of specific sections within publications: *The Washington Post's Style section, Newsweek's Periscope, Business Day.* He overhauled The Post's Sports section. Lowercase general references: *He never reads the sports section. Most business sections are boring.*

d. For style on musical compositions, see MUSIC.

e. For style on exhibitions, shows etc., see SHOWS AND EXHIBITIONS.

2. Documents, doctrines, legislation etc.
    a. Capitalize historic documents, historic doctrines, important legal codes, enacted laws, ratified treaties and ratified constitutional amendments: *Magna Carta, Mayflower Compact, Sykes-Picot Agreement, Monroe Doctrine, Taft-Hartley Act, Treaty of Versailles, Uniform Code of Military Justice, Marshall Plan, the 18th Amendment.*

    b. Lowercase general references, unratified treaties and amendments, plurals and unofficial descriptions: *President Reagan's proposed balanced-budget amendment; welfare reform bill, Kemp-Roth bill, Boland amendment, federal copyright law, First and Fifth amendments, SALT II treaty.* But capitalize *Equal Rights Amendment* even though it was not adopted.

3. **Geography, place names and natural features**

   a. Names of countries, cities, counties, provinces, states, bodies of water, mountains, valleys, deserts, structures etc. are proper nouns and are capitalized. For places and natural features not listed in this stylebook, see GEOGRAPHIC NAMES. See also FOREIGN NAMES.

   b. For adjectives derived from nouns of place or direction, generally follow the style of Webster's New World Dictionary: *Western movie, Western saddle, a western exposure; Oriental rug; southern accent, eastern styles, Eastern Shore, an easterner.* Capitalize the following well-known and commonly used names that include adjectives and descriptive features: *Northern Virginia, Southern California, East Side and West Side of Manhattan, Lower East Side, Upstate New York, South Side, North Side and Near North Side of Chicago, South Pacific, North Atlantic, South Atlantic, West Bank, Michigan's Upper Peninsula, Florida Panhandle, Great Plains, Mekong Delta, Mississippi Delta, Pacific Coast* (the region, not the shoreline), *Western Europe, Middle East, Eastern Europe, Southeast Asia, South of France, Far East, Far West.* Also capitalize *West* and *Western* in political usage: *the Western alliance, Western diplomats.*

   c. Capitalize *East, South* etc. as nouns meaning specific places or cultures: *People in the West don't understand Islam. He expects to carry most of the South.* Lowercase such terms when they are used merely as directional indicators or locators: *wind from the west, eastern Montana, central Dallas, a view toward the south, the continental shelf, upper Montgomery County, the inner city.*

   d. Capitalize fanciful terms for geographic and natural features, specific neighborhoods etc.: *Down East, Back Bay, Bible Belt, French Quarter, Oil Patch, Combat Zone, Down*

Under. Lowercase general descriptive terms that apply to more than one place: *downtown, red-light district, skid row.*

e. Lowercase generic plurals: *Montgomery and Prince George's counties; the Chesapeake and Delaware bays.*

f. Capitalize specific buildings and structures and well-known or historic places: *National Airport, Memorial Bridge, George Washington Parkway, Memorial Stadium, Chesapeake Bay Bridge, Empire State Building, National Zoo, St. Lawrence Seaway, Oval Office, Old City, Suez Canal, Hoover Dam.*

g. Capitalize the short form of specific roads and bridges after first reference: *Chesapeake Bay Bridge, the Bay Bridge; Capital Beltway, the Beltway.* Lowercase the short forms of buildings and institutions and other generic terms: *Memorial Stadium, the stadium; Chesapeake Bay, the bay; Library of Congress, the library; Georgetown University, the university; the Washington Monument, the monument.*

h. Capitalize alliances, blocs and similar groupings: *European Community, the Commonwealth, Eastern Bloc, Warsaw Pact, Organization of American States, Alliance for Progress.*

i. Capitalize administrative and political districts: *Ward 4, 18th Congressional District.*

j. Capitalize fanciful names: *Iron Curtain, Third World,* Rust Belt.*

4. **Governmental organizations**
    a. Capitalize proper or commonly accepted names for governmental organizations at all levels, including short forms and including ad hoc or temporary bodies. *U.N. Security Council, the Security Council, Foreign Ministry, Defense Department, General Assembly, Office of Technology Assessment, Board of Education, School Board* (when it is a proper name, as in *Fairfax County School Board*), *Supreme Soviet, U.N.*

Truce Supervisory Organization, Pay Board, Montgomery County Council, Warren Commission. See also CABINET.

b. Capitalize informal names: *Ex-Im Bank, the Fed, the Hill, the Pentagon.*

c. Divisions, sections and bureaus within larger organizations are capitalized when standing alone if they are identifiable without reference to the parent organization, lowercase when they are not: *the Secret Service; the Labor Department's Bureau of Labor Statistics, the Bureau of Labor Statistics; Federal Maritime Administration, the Justice Department's antitrust division, the pest management section of the Maryland Department of Agriculture, Yale Law School, the Wharton School, the Alexandria Police ballistics unit.*

d. Capitalize second references when they approximate the full name: *the National Park Service, the Park Service; the Fairfax County Board of Supervisors, the County Board; the National Weather Service, the Weather Service.* Lowercase generic terms, partial references standing alone and informal terms: *the assembly, the board, the bureau, the committee; the administration, the legislature, the lower house, the appellate court, the administration.*

e. Lowercase informal names of legislative committees and names of subcommittees except for words referring to the parent committee: *Senate rackets committee, Senate Judiciary subcommittee on refugees. Senate Agriculture Committee, Senate Agriculture subcommittee on tobacco.*

f. Lowercase such words as *city, state* and *federal* when they stand alone or are merely adjectives. Capitalize when they are part of an official name or legal entity: *Montgomery County, the Montgomery County Board, the county government; the city water supply, the City of Richmond filed suit; the federal* *government, the Federal Housing Administration; Washington state.*

g. Lowercase derivatives and adjectives unless part of a proper name. *Congressional Record, congressional apathy, senatorial courtesy.*

h. Lowercase concepts as distinct from programs and agencies that administer them. *The Federal Highway Administration runs the federal highway program.*

i. See also CABINET.

5. **Military services**
    a. Capitalize full and short names of American military services. *U.S. Army, a Navy jet, the Marine Corps, the National Guard.* See also ARMY; ARMY RESERVE and MARINE CORPS.

    b. Capitalize the proper or official names of foreign forces but lowercase generic terms and plurals. *Israeli Defense Force, Israeli army; Royal Air Force, the British air force; the People's Liberation Army, the Chinese and Soviet armies.*

    c. Capitalize specific bases, commands, units, schools and ships. *Carlisle Barracks, Andrews Air Force Base, USS Constellation, 6th Fleet, Charlie Company, Americal Division.*

    d. Capitalize fanciful and descriptive names for units. *Green Berets, Hell on Wheels, Blue Angels, Bengal Lancers.*

    e. Capitalize service and rank preceding a name. *Air Force Lt. Col. Mary White; Midshipman John Black; Marine Sgt. James Williams.* See MILITARY RANKS AND TITLES.

    f. Capitalize major wars, battles and revolts and the names of important positions and fronts, in both formal and informal designations. *Vietnam War, World War II, Korean War, Russian Revolution, Boxer Rebellion, Maginot Line, Tet Offensive, Six-Day War, Battle of the Bulge.*

g. Lowercase references to individuals unless the reference incorporates the name of the service or unit. *Army Reservist, artilleryman, ranger, paratrooper, a Green Beret, a Marine; a reservist.* See also MARINES and ARMY RESERVE.

h. Capitalize the names of weapons and aircraft. See WEAPONS AND WEAPONS SYSTEMS.

6. **Politics and political parties**

a. Capitalize political and quasi-political organizations and movements. *Democratic Party, Communist Party, New Left, National Liberation Front.* Lowercase descriptive terms not designating specific groups: *far right, pro-choice, neo-liberal, supply-siders.* When in doubt, follow the style given in Webster's New World Dictionary. See also COMMUNIST.

b. Capitalize conventions, principal bodies and officers. *Democratic National Convention, Republican Platform Committee, Communist Party Central Committee, Democratic National Chairman John Williams.* Lowercase general references: *Every Democratic convention is disorganized.*

c. Capitalize fanciful names for specific groups, places and programs. *Solid South, Grand Old Party, New Deal, New Frontier, Young Turks.* Lowercase nonspecific references: *silent majority, senior citizens.*

d. Capitalize members or adherents of a party or movement, as distinct from the philosophy or form of government. *Democrats, Republicans, Socialists, Laborites, Communists* (in specific references to members of a communist party, as in *Italy's Communists gained five seats*). But *democratic principles, conservative thinker, neo-Nazi, right-winger, leftist, communist countries. She thought every opponent of the war was a communist sympathizer.*

e. Capitalize the party-geographic designations of elected officials: *Rep. Constance A. Morella (R-Md.); D.C. Council member Joan Green (Statehood-At Large).*

7. **History and religion**

a. Capitalize eras, epochs and historic events, including wars and battles: *Dark Ages, Renaissance, Civil War, Battle of Antietam, Spanish Civil War, Jazz Age, Cultural Revolution, Beer Hall Putsch, Age of Discovery, Protestant Reformation, Great Depression.*

b. Capitalize historic and traditional addresses: *Gettysburg Address, "Cross of Gold" Speech, State of the Union Message, Sermon on the Mount.*

c. Capitalize holidays, holy days and other special days: *Independence Day, the Fourth of July; Labor Day, Mardi Gras, Martin Luther King Jr. Day, Bastille Day, Election Day, Christmas, Passover, Ramadan, Inauguration Day, New Year's Eve.* Lowercase *day, eve* etc. if not part of the holiday's name: *Thanksgiving day, Election eve.*

d. Capitalize proper nouns referring to the divinity and the Devil. *God, Allah, Jehovah; Satan, Lucifer.* Lowercase generic references: *a Greek god, the little devils.*

e. Capitalize personal pronouns referring to the deity and Jesus. Lowercase relative and possessive pronouns. *He, Thou, Him; O Thou who created all things. Christians believe He died for our sins.*

f. Capitalize the names of all recognized faiths, their adherents and their churches. Follow dictionary style on capitalization of rites and ceremonies: *last rites, Mass, bar mitzvah, Eucharist.* See also RELIGION AND THE CLERGY.

8. **Miscellaneous**

a. For proper names that have acquired independent meaning, follow the style of Webster's New World Dictionary: *Scotch whisky, portland cement, Bermuda shorts, French doors, diesel engine, a quisling.* Exceptions: *french fries,* molotov cocktail.**

b. Capitalize proper names assigned to systems and methodologies: *degrees Fahrenheit, degrees Celsius, Goren point-count system, Koechel listing, Richter scale.*

c. Capitalize designating terms used before figures and letters, except size: *Vitamin B, Room 306, Figure 3, Route 128, Model T, Division II. He wore size 38 suits; she's now a size 8.* See also NUMBER ONE.

d. Capitalize the first word of a quotation when it is a full sentence or thought, except when the quoted material is constructed to be part of the sentence. *Who said, "All that glitters is not gold"? She said she wouldn't enter because "there's no way I can win."*

e. For capitalization of acronyms, see ACRONYMS.

f. Capitalize proper adjectives in breeds of animals but lowercase the noun: *Airedale terrier, Shetland pony, German shepherd, Poland China hogs; quarter horse, thoroughbred horse, Arabian horse; fox terrier, golden retriever.*

g. Lowercase government, trade and professional terms not commonly accepted as proper nouns, even if known by initials: *consumer price index, gross national product (GNP), home edition, Dow Jones industrial average.*

h. When a full name contains a particle, follow the style of the full name when the name is used alone. The particle is generally lowercase in foreign names. It often is capitalized in anglicized names. Consult the News Library for preferred usage: *Charles de Gaulle, de Gaulle; Fiorello La*

*Guardia, La Guardia, La Guardia Airport; Rep. E. "Kika"
de la Garza, de la Garza; Herbert von Karajan, von Karajan.*
At the beginning of a sentence, such particles are always
capitalized: *Von Karajan led the orchestra.*

i. trade names. See TRADE NAMES AND BRANDS.

j. titles. See TITLES and RELIGION AND THE CLERGY.

captions

a. Whenever possible, all persons in a photo should be identified, at least by group or association if not by name:
Mayor Barry with Dunbar High School students. If a person
clearly visible in a photo cannot be identified, say so. *Mayor
Barry with Dunbar High School students and unidentified woman.
Mayor Barry with Dunbar High School students. Woman at
left is unidentified.*

b. Photo captions assume that the action took place yesterday
and are in the present tense unless some other specific time
in the past is mentioned. *President Bush greets senators at
bill-signing ceremony. John Black heads out to sea despite threat
of tropical storm.* But: *President Bush smiled as he greeted senators
at bill-signing ceremony in April. John Black headed out to sea
Thursday despite threat of tropical storm.*

c. Captions identifying more than two persons use the form
from left, not *left to right*. *Left-right* and *from left* designations
are omitted when obvious—a man with a woman, a black
person with a Chinese official etc. *President Reagan with
British Prime Minister Margaret Thatcher at Camp David,* not
President Reagan, left, with . . .

d. Keep details such as death tolls or election results out of
a caption so it does not have to be updated.

e. When a photo is old—generally five years or more—specify. *John Williams in a 1970 photo.* The time should be specified whenever a subject's appearance is known to have changed since the photo was taken, as with young people, men who have grown beards etc.

f. Avoid the term *looks on.* It is a hackneyed and lazy term, and it is something people rarely do. They watch, they listen etc.

carat, caret, carrot, karat
A *carat* is a unit of weight for gems. A *caret* is a copy editor's mark. A *carrot* is a vegetable. A *karat* is a measure of fineness in gold.

cardinal
See RELIGION AND THE CLERGY.

caster, castor
A *caster* is a wheel for furniture or a small container for condiments. *Castor* is an ingredient in perfume. *Castor oil* is a laxative.

catalogue*

catch-up
Hyphenate the noun and adjective: *They had to play catch-up. They aren't good at catch-up ball.* As a verb, catch up: *I'll catch up with you at the airport.*

Catholic religious titles
See RELIGION AND THE CLERGY.

Catholic University
The official name is the Catholic University of America. *Catholic University* is acceptable in all references.

celebrant

A celebrant is one who performs a religious rite: *At the funeral Mass, Archbishop Michael Smith was the celebrant.* The word should not be used to mean revelers or celebrators.

Celsius

This is the internationally approved designation for the metric temperature scale. (Anders Celsius was the Swedish astronomer who designed it.) Do not use *centigrade*. Temperatures are designated *38 degrees Celsius* or *38C*. Ordinarily, however, Fahrenheit temperatures are used in news stories.

center

As a verb, it is followed by on, not around. *The debate centered on U.S. policy in the region.*

Centers for Disease Control

As with the National Institutes of Health, the name is plural because there is more than one institute, although all are in the same place—in this case, Atlanta. The first reference is *Centers for Disease Control.* On second reference, give the specific center where the research is being done or the inquiry conducted.

chairman, chairwoman, chair

When referring to a specific individual, use *chairman* unless a particular woman prefers *chairwoman* or the official title of a position specifies another word. *Commodity Futures Trading Commission Chairman Wendy Gramm; Katharine Graham, chairman of the board of The Washington Post Co.; Tom Smith, chair of Citizens Against Sexism* (only if the group's bylaws make that the official title.) In general references, use *chairman. The committee will meet Tuesday to elect a chairman. Chair* may be used as a transitive verb. *She chaired a meeting of all the donor organizations.* See also SEXISM AND SEX-BASED LANGUAGE.

chaise longue; not chaise lounge.

Charles Town Race Course (West Virginia)

Charleston, W. Va. (the state capital); *Charleston,* S.C.; *Charles Town,* W.Va. (small town near Harpers Ferry).

chateau, chateaus*

chief justice
The title is chief justice of the United States, not chief justice of the Supreme Court. Before a name, capitalize and use *Chief Justice* only. *He called for the impeachment of Chief Justice Earl Warren. Earl Warren was governor of California before he became chief justice of the United States.* See also COURTS AND LEGAL TERMINOLOGY.

Chief of Staff
Capitalize as a title for the White House official and for the senior officer of the Army and the Air Force. The senior officer of the Navy is the chief of naval operations. The senior officer of the Marine Corps is the commandant. Both are capitalized as titles. See also JOINT CHIEFS OF STAFF.

Children's Hospital
Omit the words *National Medical Center.*

China
There is only one China, the People's Republic of China. *China* may be used on all references. Avoid the terms *mainland China, Communist China* and *Red China* except in historical references. For Nationalist China, use *Taiwan.*

Chinese words and names

The Pinyin transliteration is used for the names of places and persons within the People's Republic of China: *Beijing; Xinjiang province; Deng Xiaoping; sichuan cuisine*. Outside China—in Hong Kong, Singapore, Taiwan etc.—follow local preference, which often is for the old Wade-Giles transliterations: *Chiang Ching-kuo*. The family name, used on second reference, is the first name: *Deng Xiaoping, Deng; Chiang Ching-kuo, Chiang*. Wade-Giles is used for Chinese Americans and for Chinese words that are commonly recognized in English: *Cantonese cuisine, shantung silk*. For place names, consult the National Geographic Atlas.

chord, cord

A *chord* is a combination of notes in music, or a straight line joining two points in a curve. A *cord* is a rope, or a part of the anatomy, as in vocal cord, or a stack of wood measuring 4 feet by 4 feet by 8 feet.

citizens band*

classic, classical

Classic means model in nature or conforming to a recognized standard of excellence or acceptance. *Classical* refers to serious musical compositions and to certain historical periods, especially the ages of ancient Greece and Rome.

clergy

A collective noun. Do not use with a number, such as *15 clergy*. Make it *15 members of the clergy,* unless all are men, in which case *15 clergymen* is acceptable. See also RELIGION AND THE CLERGY.

co-

See PREFIXES. Note that *co-* is often redundant, as in: *One co-con-*

spirator was John Smith or *The bill's cosponsors included five Democrats.* Do not use *coequal.*

cohort

A *cohort* is a group, not an individual, as in *the Spanish-speaking cohort of the population.* The *co-* is part of the root, not a prefix. The word should not be used as a synonym for companion or colleague.

Cole Field House at the University of Maryland

collaborate, collude, connive, conspire

To *collaborate* is to work together, usually openly. To *collude* is to cooperate secretly for a deceitful purpose. To *connive* is to wink at or provide secret indulgence or assistance. To *conspire* is to plot with others to commit an illegal act.

collective nouns

Nouns that signify groups of people can be troublesome.

   a. Most collective nouns are considered singular, even though they signify more than one person: *crew, team, militia, audience, jury, family. The Harvard crew is having a good year. The militia is disorganized. The jury is still out. That family is important to its community.* These nouns have plural forms, which naturally take plural verbs. *The Harvard and Yale crews tied for first. The militias were disorganized. The juries are still out. Those families are important to their communities.*

   b. More problematic are collective nouns that are considered plural, notably *police* and *personnel.* They take plural verbs. *The police are calling it murder. Their personnel are superior to ours.*

   c. In neither group can individual members be quantified. Do not write *three crew, six police, five clergy, 13 Navy per-*

sonnel. Use *three crew members, six police officers, five members of the clergy, 13 sailors, 13 Navy employees.*

collide, collision

Two moving objects collide. A car strikes a tree; it does not collide with a tree. Do not write *was in collision with*; use *collided with*.

collude

See COLLABORATE.

colon

The colon is used to emphasize the material that follows: a list, an example, an amplification or a quotation.

a. Use a colon to introduce lists, tabulations, texts etc. *He made four points:. . . ; The opera's cast:. . .*

b. Use a colon before a direct quotation of two or more sentences. Before a one-sentence quotation, use a comma.

c. Use a colon when a quotation is introduced by a full sentence. *The president put it this way: "We will win tomorrow." The president said, "We will win tomorrow."*

d. Use a colon in script-type dialogue.

JONES: *Did you do it?*
SMITH: *I refuse to answer.*
Q: *How old are you?*
A: *I'm 25 years old.*

e. A verb before a colon is often unnecessary. *The guests at the dinner:* (Not *The guests at the dinner were:*)

f. Use a colon before a final clause summarizing preceding matter: *To be born, to live, to die: That is our fate.*

g. Use a colon in biblical citations. *Matthew 2:6.*

h. Use colons to separate hours, minutes and whole seconds in clock time and elapsed time. *It was 10:33 p.m. He ran the mile in 3:59.6.*

i. The word following a colon is capitalized in headlines. In text, it is capitalized if the colon is followed by a complete sentence. *His problem: He had more than he could use. Her problem was this: She had more than she could use. His problems were many: illness, poverty, hunger.*

comma

The comma is used to clarify text by separating groups of words or phrases. It is impossible to specify every construction in which a comma should be used. Often, reading a sentence aloud is helpful in deciding where a comma is needed to indicate a pause required for comprehension. In general, commas are used:

a. To separate words or simple phrases in a series but not before the conjunction: *red, white, green and blue; Chapter 1, 2 or 3; He packed his bags, said goodbye to his mother and rode off.*

b. To set off words in apposition—that is, words that are identifiers and if omitted from a sentence would still leave it grammatically correct: *Secretariat, the favorite, was scratched. The favorite, Secretariat, was scratched. He was there with his wife, Linda, and his oldest daughter, Sue. Her only book, "Gone With the Wind," was a blockbuster.*

c. To introduce a one-sentence direct quote: *He said, "I sure am hungry."* Do not use a comma before an indirect quote. *He said he was hungry.* Before a quote of more than one sentence, use a colon.

d. To end a quote that normally would end in a period: *"I sure am hungry," he said.* Omit the comma after a quoted sentence that ends in an exclamation point, question mark or ellipsis. *"Boy, am I hungry!" he shouted. "Am I hungry or just bored?" he wondered.* Put commas inside quotation marks, single and double.

e. To set off a quoted proper noun or book title that ends in a punctuation mark: *They performed "Oklahoma!," Rodgers and Hammerstein's musical. She was reading "What Is to Be Done?," the famous tract by Lenin.*

f. To separate two independent clauses (two full sentence patterns) that are joined by a conjunction: *He took the food out of the oven, and he dished it out to his family.* However, a comma is often unnecessary between two short independent clauses joined by a conjunction. *Now you see him and now you don't.* The comma is generally omitted between two clauses if either is not a full sentence pattern. *He took the food out of the oven and dished it out to his family.*

g. After an introductory phrase of more than a few short words: *In the last months of his reign, he became increasingly disoriented.* But *Today I'm going shopping. In 1966 he graduated from college.*

h. To set off terms of address: *No, Billy, you can't go.*

i. To indicate omission of a word or words: *Then, we had everything; now, nothing.*

j. To set off figures in apposition: *The House vote, 202 to 201, was a cliffhanger. The Cowboys turned the tables on the Cardinals, 24–7.* But *The House voted 202 to 201 against the bill. The Cowboys beat the Cardinals 24–7.*

k. In numbers higher than 999 but not in addresses, phone numbers, serial numbers etc.: *1,234 horses; 1234 Oak St.; The serial number was 123456.*

l.   After the day and year in precise dates. Omit commas when only the month and day or month and year are used. *She was born Jan. 24, 1966. She was born in January 1966.*

m.   Around the name of a state or country when it is preceded by the name of a town or other geographical designation: *The Enid, Okla., native. He was born in Enid, Okla. He lives in Oklahoma.*

n.   Before designations of academic and professional degrees and of religious orders: *John Black, MD; the Rev. Timothy Healy, SJ.*

Commas are generally not used:

a.   Before *Sr., Jr., Inc.* and *Ltd.*, before *etc.* and before Roman numerals. *Queen Elizabeth II, Acme Products Inc., Sammy Davis Jr.*

b.   In multi-unit measures of height, weight, time, latitude etc. *She stood 5 feet 6; the baby weighed 9 pounds 2 ounces; the ship was at 40 degrees 19 minutes west.*

c.   Around *of* phrases when referring to someone's title rather than residence or place of employment. *Queen Elizabeth of England* (not *Queen Elizabeth, of England*); *John Jones, of Derby, England* (not *John Jones of Derby, England*); *Chairman John Black of Acme Corp.; John Black, of Acme Corp.; Mary Smith, of 1234 Oak St., Silver Spring.*

d.   Around restrictive clauses and phrases. A clause is restrictive if its omission would alter the meaning of the sentence. If the meaning of a sentence would not be distorted by the omission of the clause, it is a nonrestrictive clause and should be set off by commas. *Reporters who fabricate quotes should be punished.* In this sentence, the clause *who fabricate quotes* is restrictive because it is essential to the meaning of the sentence. Therefore it takes no commas. The sentence means that only reporters who fabricate quotes should be punished. *Reporters, who fabricate quotes, should be punished.* Because the clause in this sentence has been set off as an appositive, the sentence implies that all reporters should be punished and all reporters fabricate quotes. *Who fabricate quotes* is a nonrestrictive modifier, set off by commas.

e. Before or after *too. I want one too. She too is running for delegate.*

Common Market
See EUROPEAN COMMUNITY.

communist
Capitalize only in specific reference to a political party. *He said he was not a communist. Gus Hall is the Communist candidate. She joined the Communist Party in 1935.* In communist countries where the ruling or official party has a euphemistic name such as People's Socialist Party, capitalize *Communist* in references to this party. *Poland is run by the Communist Party.*

compare to, compare with
In general, *compare to* stresses similarities, *compare with* stresses differences: *The candidate compared his policy to that of President Kennedy. His opponents said that compared with Kennedy, he was a lightweight.*

compendium
A *compendium* is a summary or abstract—not a complete collection.

competency
This variant spelling of *competence* should be used only in direct quotation and in citations of specific uses by others, usually educators: *The District's competency-based curriculum.*

compliment, complement
To *compliment* is to praise. To *complement* is to complete or enhance.

compound words
For compound words not listed in this stylebook, follow the style given in Webster's New World Dictionary: *Lifestyle*, but *life raft; backstop*, but *back talk, back yard, back seat; ballhandler, ballhawk*, but *ball carrier, ball bearing* etc. Exception: *ballclub*.* For compounds not listed here or in the dictionary, observe the following guidelines:

a.   The first objective always is clarity. Regardless of any other rule, use a hyphen if its omission could confuse the reader. For example, a hyphen is generally not required in a compound consisting of two nouns: *box office success, sewage treatment plant*. But in this headline it is essential: *Rescue Squad Helps Dog-Bite Victims*.

b.   When the compound precedes a noun generally use a hyphen between an adjective and a noun, between an adjective and a verb, between a noun and an adjective or participle and between a verb and a preposition: *a first-rate play; far-reaching legislation; large-scale project; beefed-up security; record-breaking speed, tax-free zone, drug-related death*.

c.   Some adjective-noun phrases are so commonly used that hyphens are not needed. Editors must use their judgment about which expressions fall into this category. Among them certainly are *Social Security benefits, acid rain legislation, high school student, dining room table, light blue dress, Washington area charities*.

d.   If a modifier preceding a noun consists of several words, all must be hyphenated unless the noun phrase is capitalized. It is best to avoid an unwieldy string of modifiers by placing the compound after the noun as an unhyphenated phrase.

POOR: *abortion-on-demand opponents; the Nobel Peace Prize-winning Kissinger; She received an almost-too-good-to-be-true windfall.*

BETTER: *opponents of abortion on demand; Kissinger, winner of the Nobel Peace Prize; Her windfall seemed almost too good to be true.*

e.   Do not hyphenate a compound in which the first element is an adverb ending in *ly*. *His eagerly awaited arrival; a totally inept performance.* But note that some adjectives end in *ly*. Those words are hyphenated in compounds: *A scholarly-looking man.*

f.   Modifiers in which the first element is *well* are hyphenated before the noun but not after. *A well-acted play; the play was well acted.*

g.   Compound modifiers containing the adverbs *very, already, more, most* and *less* are not hyphenated except when necessary for clarity. *The already tired committee; the more favored few.* But note the distinction between *The soup kitchen feeds the most hungry men* and *The soup kitchen feeds the most-hungry men.*

h.   Other compounds containing comparatives and superlatives are hyphenated when they precede the noun: *the fastest-growing city, a slower-moving bureaucracy.*

i.   Do not hyphenate compound proper adjectives or compound proper nouns used as modifiers unless the first element ends in *-o* or the nouns designate a joint relationship: *Italian American neighborhood; Franco-Prussian War; Sino-Soviet agreement; U.S.-Canada trade pact.*

j.   Foreign phrases used as modifiers are not hyphenated unless the dictionary specifies otherwise. *per capita spending; ad hoc committee; laissez-faire attitude.*

k. Retain hyphens in suspended compounds, those in which the basic element is omitted after all but the last term: *5-, 10- and 20-foot sections.*

l. Hyphenate compound modifiers that have an apostrophe in the first element: *bull's-eye aim; camel's-hair brush.*

m. Many compounds with *over-* and *under-* are in the dictionary. Follow dictionary style. For those not listed in the dictionary, hyphenate those with roots of three or more syllables. Do not hyphenate those with roots of one or two syllables, *overeducated, underfed, underexposed.*

comprise

The word means contain or consist of. The whole comprises the parts, not vice versa. *The alphabet comprises 26 letters.* Do not say *The alphabet is comprised of 26 letters.*

computer language

a. The era of the personal computer has introduced a whole new glossary of words and acronyms into the language. Many of these—ASCII, dot-matrix, FORTRAN, megabyte—are listed in Webster's New World Dictionary, third edition, and may be used in the forms given there. The 1987 edition of the Associated Press stylebook, available in the News Library, provides an excellent list of computer terms and their definitions.

b. In general, computer terms should be explained for the benefit of readers unfamiliar with them. Computer-related acronyms such as *ROM* (read-only memory), *RAM* (random-access memory), *DOS* (disk operating system) and *LAN* (local area network) should be spelled out on first reference or given in apposition.

c. Abbreviations expressing storage or memory capacity, such as *k* for *kilobyte,* may be used on second reference. *That old*

*computer had only 128 kilobytes of random access memory (RAM).
Her new one has 640k.* See ABBREVIATIONS, 1a.

condominium

The word is frequently misused. Condominium is a form of property
ownership, not a type of structure. An apartment may or may not
be a condominium. A condominium community is one in which
occupants own their individual dwellings or offices but the hallways
and exterior areas are held in common. It may consist of high-rise
apartments, garden apartments, town houses, offices or all four. To
say *She lives in a condominium in Miami* does not convey any information about the type of dwelling she lives in or her financial
arrangements—she may be renting it from the owner. Use *apartment,
town house* etc. Restrict *condo* to jocular usage and quotations.

congressman, congresswoman

This is not a title and is not capitalized. In theory, the term is
applicable to any member of the House or Senate, but in practice
it is applied only to representatives. Use the correct titles, *Senator*
and *Representative*, for the abbreviations, with the names of individuals. *Congressman*, meaning member of the U.S. House, is acceptable
in a sentence such as *The protesters marched to the congressman's office*,
when the person is in fact male, otherwise use *congresswoman*.

connive

See COLLABORATE.

conspire

See COLLABORATE.

continual, continuous

Continual means constantly repeated. *Continuous* means uninter-
rupted. *The continual pounding of the drum. Two days of continuous
debate.*

contractions

Contractions use the apostrophe to indicate omitted letters: *can't, wouldn't, it's.* Contractions convey an informal tone more appropriate for feature stories and commentary than for straight news. In any type of story, however, contractions are used in quotations when the speaker actually used them.

convince, persuade

Convince takes *of* or *that*, *persuade* takes the infinitive. *He convinced her of his sincerity. He convinced her that she should believe him. He persuaded her to believe him.*

copyright

Noun, verb and adjective: *a copyright article*, not *copyrighted*.

corporate names

a. Standard & Poor's Register of Corporations is the authority for names of corporations. Privately held corporations not listed by Standard & Poor's may be found in the Million Dollar Directory, published by Dun & Bradstreet.

b. Names of corporations are capitalized and given in full on first reference: *International Business Machines Corp., General Motors Corp., Potomac Electric Power Co.* In subsequent references they may be abbreviated: *IBM, GM, Pepco.* In headlines, use abbreviations for corporations that are widely known, such as IBM, GM, 3M, and for those that have adopted initials as their official names: CSX, USX, USF&G. For lesser-known companies or companies that have changed their names recently to initial style, include the original name on an early reference. *CBI Industries Inc., formerly Chicago Bridge & Iron Co.*

c. Capitalize *The* only in The Washington Post Co.

d. Follow corporate style on punctuation, the ampersand etc., but do not use a comma before *Inc., & Co.* etc. *Time Inc.; Ferris & Co. Inc.; Archer-Daniels-Midland Co.*

e. On corporate names made from acronyms, capitalize the first letter only: *Geico, Pepco, Nabisco, Alcoa.*

council, counsel, consul
A *council* is a deliberative body, as in City Council. *Counsel* is advice or one who gives advice, usually legal advice. A *consul* is a diplomatic official. *The consul from the French Embassy sought counsel about his testimony before the City Council.*

counter-
See PREFIXES.

couple
The word is usually plural. *The couple were rich, but they were unhappy. He had most of the parts, but a couple of them were missing.* The word takes a singular verb when it emphasizes the unit: *One couple went skiing but the other was determined to go someplace warm. Couple* requires *of* before a noun. *A couple of problems,* not *a couple problems.*

Court House (Virginia Metro station)

court-martial (noun and verb)
The plural is courts-martial.

Court of St. James's*
The official name of the British royal court.

courts and legal terminology
The Washington Metropolitan Area comprises two states with dif-

ferent court systems and the District of Columbia, which has overlapping federal and local jurisdiction.

a.   In all stories involving judges and legal proceedings, specify the court in which the proceedings take place and name the presiding judge or magistrate. When appellate courts issue rulings, name the judge who wrote the opinion and the other members of the panel.

b.   In general, federal courts handle criminal cases involving violations of federal law, such as interstate kidnapping, mail fraud, robbery of a federally insured bank and income tax evasion. They also handle civil actions involving federal jurisdiction and constitutional issues, such as regulation of interstate commerce and the protection of individuals against violation of their civil rights.

c.   Bankruptcy proceedings are also federal cases but they are conducted in a separate court. See BANKRUPTCY.

d.   The vast majority of criminal cases, including most murders, rapes and robberies, and all civil cases that do not involve federal issues, such as zoning or contract disputes, are heard in state courts. These are called trial courts, courts in which juries are empaneled and trials are conducted. The trial court in Maryland and Virginia is the circuit court—Montgomery County Circuit Court, Fairfax County Circuit Court etc. In the District of Columbia, the trial court is the D.C. Superior Court. In New York, it is the State Supreme Court.

e.   D.C. Superior Court is the forum for all non-federal cases in the District of Columbia, from traffic cases and minor contract disputes to felonies and major challenges to mayoral authority. In Maryland and Virginia, there is a system of lower courts below the trial court level where misde-

meanors and minor civil cases are heard and where pre-
liminary proceedings in felony cases are handled before
the cases go to a circuit court. In Maryland, these are
district courts. In Virginia, they are general district courts.

f.   The names of specific courts are capitalized, general ref-
     erences are lowercase: *He was a judge in the U.S. District
     Court in Baltimore. She said he would be tried in another circuit
     court in Maryland. Fairfax County General District Court
     Judge Ann Brown resigned yesterday. All U.S. courts of appeals
     have crowded dockets. She was named a judge of the U.S. Tax
     Court.*

g.   Federal courts are organized into districts and circuits,
     which are groups of districts. All of Maryland is one
     federal court district. The main courthouse is in Balti-
     more. In Virginia, there are two districts, Eastern and
     Western. The cities and counties of the Washington sub-
     urbs are in the Eastern District. The main courthouse is
     in Richmond, but most cases from Northern Virginia are
     heard in a branch courthouse in Alexandria. Appeals from
     U.S. district court rulings in both states are heard by the
     U.S. Court of Appeals for the 4th Circuit, or the 4th
     U.S. Circuit Court of Appeals, based in Richmond. The
     District of Columbia is a single district and a single cir-
     cuit. The U.S. Court of Appeals for the District of Co-
     lumbia Circuit (or, informally, D.C. Circuit) hears appeals
     from federal court rulings in the District of Columbia, as
     well as appeals of rulings by U.S. government agencies.

h.   A judge in a U.S. district court is *U.S. District Judge Mary
     Jones* (not *U.S. District Court Judge Mary Jones*); *a U.S.
     district judge. The trial was held in U.S. District Court in
     San Francisco. U.S. District Judge George Brown presided.* A
     judge in a U.S. circuit court of appeals is *U.S. Appeals*

Court Judge Mary Jones or *Judge Mary Jones of the 4th U.S. Circuit Court of Appeals.* In general references, a *U.S. appellate judge, a federal appellate judge* or *a U.S. circuit court judge.*

i. Some federal cases go to courts of specialized jurisdiction.

The U.S. Claims Court hears financial claims against the federal government.

The U.S. Court of International Trade (based in New York, formerly the Court of Customs and Patent Appeals) hears customs, trade and patent disputes.

The U.S. Court of Military Appeals hears appeals from rulings of courts-martial.

The U.S. Court of Appeals for the Federal Circuit hears appeals from the specialized federal courts such as the Claims Court.

The U.S. Tax Court adjudicates disputes between the Internal Revenue Service and corporate and individual taxpayers.

See also BANKRUPTCY.

j. In the District of Columbia, a judge in Superior Court is *D.C. Superior Court Judge John Smith.* His rulings may be appealed to the D.C. Court of Appeals. Note that the D.C. Court of Appeals is a local court, equivalent to a state appellate court; it is not to be confused with the U.S. Court of Appeals for the District of Columbia, a federal court.

k. In Maryland, a judge in Circuit Court is *Montgomery County Circuit Court Judge Joan Johnson,* or *a Prince George's County Circuit Court judge*; in general references, *a circuit court judge, the state's circuit court judges.* Trial court rulings may be appealed to the Maryland Court of Special Appeals and from there to the state's highest court, the Maryland Court of Appeals.

l. In Virginia, a judge in circuit court is *Fairfax County Circuit Court Judge William Johnson* or *Alexandria Circuit Court Judge William Johnson.* His rulings may be appealed to the Court of Appeals of Virginia and from there to the Supreme Court of Virginia. Some cases go directly from circuit court to the Supreme Court of Virginia.

m. The attorney for the government—the prosecutor—in all federal courts and in D.C. Superior Court is the U.S. attorney, appointed by the president. In Maryland state courts, it is the state's attorney, an elected official. In Virginia state courts, it is the commonwealth's attorney, also elected. In most other states, it is the district attorney. These are capitalized as titles: *U.S. Attorney Michael Adams; Assistant Commonwealth's Attorney Louise Williams.* Do not abbreviate.

n. Appellate courts, including the U.S. Supreme Court, do not conduct trials or hear evidence. They consider only legal issues presented in written pleadings called briefs and in oral argument by lawyers. The U.S. Supreme Court declines to consider most cases presented to it. When it refuses to take a case, the legal effect is to leave standing the decision of the lower court. When the court does take a case, it is said to grant a *Writ of certiorari*, but it is better to write that *the Supreme Court agreed to hear* or *refused to consider* a case. See also CHIEF JUSTICE.

o. A person accused of a crime pleads *guilty* or *not guilty*. He or she does not plead *innocent*. If there is a trial, the defendant will be found *guilty* or *not guilty*. There is no verdict of *innocent*.

   Occasionally a judge will accept a plea of *nolo contendere* or no contest, in which the accused does not admit guilt but does not contest the charge. When a plea of no contest is being discussed, be sure the court accepts it before reporting that the defendant entered such a plea. See also INNOCENT, NOT GUILTY and INDICTMENT.

p. In reporting a prison sentence, such as 5 to 15 years, report also when the person will be eligible for parole: *after three years, after 18 months.*

q. The names of specific court cases are italicized: *Plessy v. Ferguson; Baker v. Carr; State of Maryland v. O'Hara.*

r. Also italicized are the words of Latin jargon common in legal proceedings: *in camera, nolle prosequi, res judicata.* It is better to use the English equivalents, but if the Latin terms must be used, as in quotations, they should be translated or explained: *in camera (in the judge's chambers); nolle prosequi (drop the charges); pro bono (free, without a fee); res judicata (already decided).* The exception is *habeas corpus,* for which there is no other term.

s. Anyone can sue any person or organization and claim any amount of damages. The amount of monetary damages claimed in a lawsuit does not add validity to the plaintiff's claim, nor does it make the claim inherently newsworthy. Most lawsuits never go to trial, and those that do rarely result in damage awards as high as the original claim. Lawyers frequently inflate the claim, knowing they will settle for less but hoping to gain publicity. Be very cautious about reporting such lawsuits. *John Smith sued the XYZ Corp. for $106 million yesterday* is eye-catching, but it may not be newsworthy. In a criminal case, the plaintiff is the government, the state, the people, and thus the actions of a prosecutor, who is the people's representative, are inherently newsworthy. In a civil lawsuit, the plaintiff could well be an irresponsible, desperate or publicity-seeking individual. See also LAWSUITS.

See also ATTORNEY, LAWYER

*couturier**

crafted, hand-crafted
Though widely accepted, these words should be used sparingly. They are pseudo-fancy synonyms for made and handmade.

crescendo
This word is often misused. It means a gradual increase in loudness or intensity, not a high point or climax. *A crescendo of protest finally forced the mayor to act.*

crew
A collective noun. Do not use with a number, such as *five crew*. Make it *five crew members*, or *a crew of five*. In sports, use *crew*, not *crew team*. *He rowed on the Cornell crew.*

criterion, criteria
A *criterion* is a standard or test by which something can be judged. It takes a singular verb. Its plural is *criteria*. *They failed because the criteria were too strict.*

critique
As a noun, a *critique* is an analysis or evaluation, not necessarily unfavorable. As a verb, *critique* means to analyze and evaluate—not necessarily unfavorably. A critique may be favorable. To critique unfavorably is to criticize.

cross, cross-
See COMPOUND WORDS. Exception: crosscheck* without the hyphen in hockey stories. *She cross-checked his footnotes against the text. He crosschecked Gretzky right in front of the referee.*

cruise missile
Always lowercase.

currency
Spell out units of currency, except for $ with units of U.S. money. Do not capitalize. Use the name of the country only for clarity: *Canadian dollar, U.S. dollar; guilder, yen; French franc, German mark* (not *deutschemark.*) Always give the U.S. dollar equivalent or some other way to understand the value. See also NUMERALS.

currently, presently
The present tense of English verbs generally speaks for itself. It means an action happening now. It is rarely necessary to reinforce the time element with adverbs such as *currently* or *presently*. *He is chairman of the committee* means what it says. It is more verbose but not more precise to say *He is currently chairman of the committee* or *He is presently a director of three corporations*. It may sometimes be necessary to use *now* to make a specific distinction from some other time: *He is now chairman of the committee but he was then its recording secretary*. Otherwise, omit the adverb. In any case, *presently* means in a little while, not at present.

curveball

dais
See PODIUM.

dark horse (noun); *dark-horse* (adjective)

dash
The dash is used to indicate abrupt changes in thought, continuity or pace. A pair of dashes can replace a pair of commas or parentheses and a single dash can replace a colon, but in general dashes should

be used sparingly because they interrupt the flow of the sentence and convey extra emphasis. No space or punctuation precedes or follows the dash.

    a. Use a dash to indicate a sharp turn in thought or a significant pause: *I'm waiting for—ah, I see her now. After three days, we found him—in jail!*

    b. In a direct quote, use dashes instead of parentheses to set off a complete sentence within another sentence. Parentheses could be misinterpreted as the writer's interpolation: *"And then my brother—he was 21 at the time—went into the Navy."*

    c. Use dashes between parts of a direct quote to interject a complete sentence: *"My only son"—his tone was grave—"is missing."*

    d. Use a dash after a dateline.

    e. Use a dash between a quotation and an author's name.

    f. Try to avoid using dashes in headlines. They are typographically unattractive.

data

The plural of *datum*, Latin for that which is given. It requires a plural verb except in quotations. *The data don't support his argument.* If uncomfortable with this, use another word: *information, numbers, survey results* etc.

datelines

    a. Datelines giving place and date are used with stories filed from outside the Washington metropolitan area: *NEW YORK, Dec. 25—; CUMBERLAND, Md., Aug. 1—.*

    b. A story filed from a dateline site on the same day the paper is published includes the day of the week: *HANOI, Feb. 16 (Thursday)—.*

c. In all datelined stories, time elements reflect filing date, not publication date. A story filed from Richmond on Jan. 30 and published in the Jan. 31 paper would say: *RICHMOND, Jan. 30—Gov. Gerald L. Baliles said today* . . . Do not use a date with the dateline on a story more than 24 hours old.

d. Do not use *yesterday* or *tomorrow* in datelined stories. Specify the day of the week. See also TIME.

e. Datelines may be used only if the person writing the story was actually present in the location on the day mentioned. If the reporter must leave a city before filing a story, as often happens during wars and political campaigns, the dateline may still be used if the reporter was in that place on that day. Stories more than 24 hours old and stories with no time element, such as features or backgrounders written after a reporter has left the city or country, may have a dateline without a date: *DAMASCUS—*

f. Datelines are used on all stories filed from places in Maryland and Virginia that are outside the Washington metropolitan area, including Baltimore, Richmond and Annapolis. In the Washington area, datelines are not used on stories filed from Montgomery, Prince George's, Howard or Charles counties in Maryland or from places in Anne Arundel County other than Annapolis. In Virginia, datelines are not used on stories from Arlington, Fairfax, Loudoun or Prince William counties or from cities within them, such as Manassas, or from Alexandria.

g. *UNITED NATIONS* and *CAPE CANAVERAL* stand alone as datelines—no state.

h. Stories filed from any of the five boroughs of New York carry the dateline *NEW YORK*, not *Brooklyn, the Bronx* etc. Stories filed from towns on Long Island carry *N.Y.,* not *L.I.: HEMPSTEAD, N.Y., April 5—*

i. Sports deadlines may use resorts, clubs or subdivisions if
    they have acquired an identity of their own: *WIMBLE-
    DON, England; FOREST HILLS, N.Y.* (for an event at
    the West Side Tennis Club; otherwise, *NEW YORK,* be-
    cause Forest Hills is inside the city); *SUN VALLEY,
    Idaho.*

j. Ships at sea may be usd as datelines: *ABOARD THE USS
    CORAL SEA, June 25—.* Military bases in the United
    States are used as datelines if they are separate geographic
    entities: *FORT DIX, N.J.,* but not *Fort Detrick,* which is
    in Frederick, Md. The test is whether the military base
    has its own Zip code.

k. Stories from Canada use the name of the province after
    the name of the city. Only British Columbia is abbrevi-
    ated: *HALIFAX, Nova Scotia; VANCOUVER, B.C.*

l. The following cities in the United States need not be
    identified by state, either in datelines or in text:

Albuquerque	Denver
Anchorage	Des Moines
Annapolis	Detroit
Atlanta	El Paso
Atlantic City	Fort Worth
Baltimore	Hartford
Birmingham	Hollywood
Boston	Honolulu
Buffalo	Houston
Charlottesville	Indianapolis
Chicago	Iowa City
Cincinnati	Jersey City
Cleveland	Las Vegas
Colorado Springs	Los Angeles
Dallas	Louisville

Memphis	Richmond
Miami	Roanoke
Miami Beach	Salt Lake City
Milwaukee	San Antonio
Minneapolis	San Diego
Nashville	San Francisco
Newark	San Jose
Norfolk	Seattle
New Orleans	St. Louis
New York	Tampa
Oakland	Toledo
Oklahoma City	Tucson
Omaha	Tulsa
Philadelphia	Virginia Beach
Phoenix	Williamsburg
Pittsburgh	

m. The following foreign cities need not be identified by country, either in datelines or text:

Algiers	Budapest
Amsterdam	Buenos Aires
Athens	Cairo
Bangkok	Calcutta
Barcelona	Copenhagen
Beijing	Dublin
Belfast	East Berlin
Belgrade	Florence
Beirut	Geneva
Bombay	Guatemala City
Bonn	The Hague
Brasilia	Hamburg
Brussels	Hanoi

Havana	Paris
Helsinki	Prague
Hong Kong	Quebec City
Istanbul	Rio de Janeiro
Jerusalem	Rome
Johannesburg	Rotterdam
Kuwait	San Salvador
Leningrad	Seoul
Lisbon	Shanghai
London	Singapore
Luxembourg	Stockholm
Madrid	Sydney
Manila	Tehran
Mexico City	Tel Aviv
Milan	Tokyo
Montreal	Toronto
Moscow	Tunis
Munich	Vatican City
Nairobi	Venice
Naples	Vienna
New Delhi	Warsaw
Oslo	West Berlin
Ottawa	Zurich
Panama City	

n. In sports stories, omit the country with the name of any city that has a franchise in a major sport, such as Calgary or Edmonton.

day care; day-care center

daylight saving time
Not *daylight savings time. Daylight saving time begins Sunday.* See also TIME.

deaf

People who cannot hear are deaf. If they are also unable to speak, they are deaf and mute. Do not use the terms *deaf mute* or *deaf and dumb*.

death penalty, death sentence

The death penalty is execution. A judge in the courtroom imposes a death sentence, not the death penalty.

debut

Debut is a noun. Some authorities accept it as a verb but only as an intransitive verb, not with a direct object.

> ACCEPTABLE: *The pianist debuted with the Cleveland Orchestra in 1985.*

> UNACCEPTABLE: *The Cleveland Orchestra debuted the concerto in 1985.*

decor*

department stores

The informal or popular names of department stores and other stores may generally be used in text, except in reference to the parent corporation. *She went shopping at Macy's. He owns stock in R.H. Macy & Co. That mall has no Sears store. She is a lawyer for Sears, Roebuck and Co.* In general, the informal names are the ones the stores use in their advertisements. Some of these take the possessive form, some do not. Some take the apostrophe, others do not. *Hecht's; Raleighs; Bloomingdale's; Lord & Taylor; Woodies; JCPenney; Hechinger.*

deprecate, depreciate

To *deprecate* is to express disapproval of or to plead against. To *depreciate* is to decline in value, to make seem less or to belittle.

detective
Do not abbreviate.

detente*

diagnose
A disease is diagnosed, not a person.

> CORRECT: *His cancer was diagnosed in 1988.*
>
> INCORRECT: *He was diagnosed with cancer in 1988.*

dialect
See QUOTATIONS.

die of (not from)

die, dye
To *die* is to cease to be alive. To *dye* is to color. A person who is deeply committed to something is said to be *dyed in the wool*. Avoid euphemisms for *die*, such as *pass away*.

dilemma
A *dilemma* is a choice between unfavorable or disagreeable alternatives. It is not a synonym for *problem*. If a synonym for *problem* is required, use *predicament* or *quandary*.

dimensions
Use figures and spell out units of measure to indicate height, depth, length, width and weight. But where the dimension has only one element, spell out whole numbers less than 10: *She is 5 feet 2 inches tall; a 6-foot-2 man; a 6-2 man; a 98-pound woman; a 9-by-12-foot rug, a 9-by-12 rug; a 50-meter pool; five inches of snow; a two-mile stretch of road, a 2.6-mile stretch of road; an 8-pound 6-ounce baby; a 2,000-square-foot house.* See also NUMERALS.

disabled

People who are permanently disabled in one way or another generally do not like to be described as handicapped. Use *disabled* or specify the nature of the disability. When a disability requires use of a wheelchair, say *uses a wheelchair*, not *confined to a wheelchair*.

> ACCEPTABLE: *She uses a wheelchair because she is disabled by muscular dystrophy.*

> UNACCEPTABLE: *She is confined to a wheelchair because she is handicapped by muscular dystrophy.*

Handicapped, however, is perfectly acceptable in describing a temporary disability: *He was handicapped by a broken collarbone.*

disc, disk

Use *disc* for the blade of the harrow and in association with sound reproduction: *compact disc, disc jockey.* All others are *disks*: *computer disks, intervertebral disks* etc.

disinterested

It means impartial or neutral. A person who is not interested is uninterested. The umpire in a baseball game is disinterested, but not necessarily uninterested.

disperse, disburse

To *disperse* is to scatter. To *disburse* is to pay out.

district attorney

Do not abbreviate.

District of Columbia

This can almost always be shortened to *D.C.* (adjective) or *the District* (noun or adjective). *The D.C. Board of Education operates the public schools in the District. He was elected to the D.C. school board. D.C. Council member Michael Jenkins complained that commuters were parking on District streets.* See also POLICE and WASHINGTON.

District of Columbia Council
The D.C. Council (not D.C. City Council); the council. *D.C. Council members Mary Brown (D-Ward 2) and Andrew White (R-At Large).*

doctor, Dr.
Do not use *Doctor* or *Dr.* as a title, except in quotations. So many types of professional persons claim the title that it conveys no information to the reader about their qualifications. Dr. Ann Brown could be a neurosurgeon, a research microbiologist, a chiropractor, a veterinarian or a specialist in early childhood education. Formerly the newspaper reserved *doctor* for "practitioners of the healing arts," excluding holders of PhD degrees. But the link between medicine and research science is now so close that this distinction is no longer valid. To avoid having to make unfair or invalid distinctions, omit the title and describe the individual: *John Williams, a clinical psychologist; Mary Andrews, a cardiologist; Michael Jones, a podiatrist.* On second reference, use last name only. Use *doctor* as a generic reference to a physician. *He wants to be a doctor. The hospital closed when all its doctors walked out.*

doughnut

Dow Jones industrial average
This is a widely used index (not really an average) of stock market activity, based on the prices of 30 blue-chip stocks. It is given in points. *The Dow Jones industrial average closed at 2042.5 points.* Informally, *the Dow* on second reference. *She said the drop in the Dow wasn't significant.*

downplay

An unnecessary neologism that should be avoided. Use *play down,* which is what it means.

drier, dryer

Drier means less moist. A *dryer* is a device for drying things.

Dulles Airport, Dulles International Airport

See WASHINGTON DULLES INTERNATIONAL AIRPORT.

Dupont Circle (Washington); E. I. du Pont de Nemours & Co.

The Du Pont Co. is acceptable on all references.

East Capitol Street

Also North and South Capitol streets. Do not abbreviate the directions. The roadbeds of North, East and South Capitol streets are not in any quadrant; they divide the quadrants. But addresses on them are in quadrants: *398 East Capitol St. NE; 3837 South Capitol St. SW.* There is no West Capitol Street. The Mall is where West Capitol Street would be.

eatery

A slang term for a lunchroom or diner. It should not be used as a synonym for *restaurant* or *cafe.*

effect

See AFFECT.

either . . . or

The expression requires a balanced construction. The same part of speech or grammatical construction must follow both words.

> CORRECT: *He was either dead or faking.*
>
> INCORRECT: *Either he was dead or faking.*

See NOT ONLY . . . BUT ALSO.

The construction *either . . . or* may not be used with more than two elements. Do not write *He can play either second base or shortstop or the outfield.*

elderly
See AGE.

ellipsis
The ellipsis (. . .) indicates the omission of words or sentences. It is used most often to remove unimportant or irrelevant matter from quotations or text. It may also be used in stylized writing to join unrelated words or sentences. The ellipsis is typeset with spaces before and after it and with thin spaces between the periods to prevent their breaking at the end of a line, but no space is set between a quotation mark and an ellipsis.

a. Use the ellipsis to indicate omissions in quotations or text. *"The first thing . . . is to hire him," Black said.*

b. When an ellipsis is used at the end of a sentence, put a period or other terminal punctuation at the end of the sentence. Never use a comma with an ellipsis. *"The first thing is to hire him. . . . Then we can deal with him," Black said. "Why don't we hire him first? . . . Then we can deal with him," Black said.*

c. It usually is unnecessary to end a quoted sentence or begin a quote with an ellipsis. See QUOTATIONS.

d. Do not use an ellipsis in place of a dash, comma or colon to indicate pauses in speech or words in apposition. It could be misinterpreted as indicating omitted material.

embassy
Capitalize with the name of a nation, lowercase without it. *The French Embassy. The building isn't suitable for an embassy.*

emigrate, immigrate

To *emigrate* (from) is to leave a country permanently. To *immigrate* (to) is to enter a country for permanent residence.

en route*

Encyclopaedia Britannica

enormity

It means great wickedness or outrageousness: *the enormity of the crime*. Something that is very big is characterized by enormousness, not necessarily by enormity.

ensure

See ASSURE.

enthuse

As a verb, this is a colloquial back formation from enthusiastic that should be avoided in standard English.

epitome

The embodiment or ideal representation of something, not a high point or climax. One's attire may be the epitome of fashion, but a triumph is not the epitome of a career.

equal

Equal is an absolute. Things are equal or not. They cannot be more equal or less equal, though they may be *more nearly equal*. Do not use *coequal*.

ethnic descriptions

See RACE AND RACIAL IDENTIFICATION. See also PHYSICAL APPEARANCE.

European Community

Not *European Economic Community* or *Common Market*. On second reference, *the Community* or *the EC*, but *EC* should be avoided in headlines because it is unfamiliar to the general reader.

ex-

Hyphenate *ex-* when it means former, as in *ex-wife*. *Ex-*, meaning former, is not used before an adjective except where necessary in headlines. In text, avoid writing *ex-French president, ex-Citicorp chairman, ex-world champion*. Use *former*. See also PREFIXES.

exclamation point

The exclamation point should be used sparingly in quotes and almost never in other text. Irony, surprise or excitement should be conveyed by the wording of the sentence, not by a typographic device.

    a. Use an exclamation point to emphasize an exclamatory tone in a quote. *"I can't believe it!" she cried.*

    b. Do not use a comma after an exclamation point unless the exclamation point is part of a proper noun rather than the ending of a sentence. *"I did it!" she shouted. "Dancin'!," at area theaters, is rated PG.*

    c. The exclamation point goes inside quotation marks only if the quote is exclamatory or contains a proper noun that includes an exclamation point. *"Look, there's that guy from 'The A-Team'!" she cried. "Oh, look, there's that guy from 'Dancin'!' "*

extra-

See PREFIXES. In quotations of colloquial speech, *extra* as a modifier is not hyphenated. *"She's extra good at that."*

*facade**

farther, further
Farther generally refers to distance. *Further* means to a greater degree. *The farther they went, the further he felt himself separated from reality.*

fastball

Father
Do not use as a title for priests. See also RELIGION AND THE CLERGY.

Federal National Mortgage Association
This is a private corporation, not a government agency. It issues securities backed by pools of mortgages. The agency may be called *Fannie Mae* on second reference and in headlines. Its bonds are *Fannie Maes. Fannie May* is a brand of candy.

feel like
The use of this expression to introduce a subordinate clause is a colloquialism that should be avoided except in quotations. *Like* is followed by a noun. *I feel like an idiot.* Incorrect: *They feel like there's no stopping them now. We feel like the verdict was unfair.* Use *think* or *believe* as the verb. Acceptable as a quotation: *"I feel like we're going to win today," he said.*

fewer
See LESS, FEWER.

fiance (man); fiancee (woman)

firearms
It is always a good idea to check the details about the caliber and firing mode of any firearm. In general: A rifle has a rifled or helical bore that causes a bullet to spin. A shotgun has a smooth bore. Rifles and pistols use cartridges as their ammunition. A cartridge

consists of a bullet and a cylindrical case. The weapons fire the bullets from the cartridges; the cases are ejected, either automatically or manually. Shotguns use shells containing shot or a single slug.

An automatic weapon is one that fires continuously as long as the trigger is being squeezed. A semiautomatic fires once each time the trigger is squeezed, without having to be recocked manually. Ammunition for an automatic or semiautomatic weapon usually is loaded from a magazine that attaches to the weapon and keeps inserting cartridges, or rounds, until it is empty.

Rifles may or may not be automatic; some can be converted from semiautomatic to automatic. An automatic rifle is not a machine gun. A machine gun is larger and is usually mounted.

Handguns may be single-shot pistols, revolvers or semiautomatics. Use *handgun* unless you know which.

The caliber of a weapon is a measurement of the inside diameter of the barrel of a pistol, rifle or artillery weapon. It may be expressed in millimeters (*a 9mm pistol, a 105mm howitzer*) or in decimal fractions of an inch (*a .45-caliber automatic; a .22-caliber rifle; a .357 magnum*). Shotgun sizes are given in gauges: *a 12-gauge shotgun, a 20-gauge shotgun.* The larger the gauge, the smaller the barrel diameter. One exception is the .410-gauge shotgun; the .410 is a caliber but it is commonly referred to as a gauge.

First Lady*
Sobriquets, including this one, are capitalized.

fiscal year
The fiscal year is the year between settlements of financial accounts. Private and governmental organizations calculate revenue and spending by fiscal year. It may coincide with the calendar year but often does not. The U.S. government's fiscal year begins Oct. 1. Fiscal 1989 (not Fiscal Year 1989) is the year ending Sept. 30, 1989. The abbreviation *FY* should be restricted to headlines and tabular matter.

flack, flak

Flack is a slang term for press agent. *Flak* is antiaircraft fire.

flaunt, flout

To *flaunt* is to display boastfully. To *flout* is to treat with disdain: *They flouted the law.*

flew, flied

The past tense of fly is flew except in baseball: *The batter flied out in the second inning.*

flounder, founder

As a verb, *flounder* means to struggle clumsily. *Founder* means to become disabled or sink.

Folger Shakespeare Library

Use this name only for the library. The theater company, which no longer has any formal connection with the library, is the Shakespeare Theatre at the Folger.

forbid

Forbid requires the infinitive form of the subsequent verb. One is forbidden to do something, not forbidden from doing it. *The general forbade the troops to carry loaded weapons on guard duty.*

Ford's Theatre

forebear, forbear

A *forebear* is an ancestor. *Forbear* means refrain.

forego, forgo

To *forego* is to precede. To *forgo* is to do without.

foreign legislatures

Use *legislature* or *parliament* for general references to the legislative bodies of foreign countries. *Israel's parliament voted yesterday to increase spending for education in the West Bank. Three socialists have been elected to the Japanese parliament.* On first reference to the specific organization, both the proper name—Israel's Knesset, Japan's Diet, West Germany's Bundestag etc.—and the generic may be used. *The whaling-rights issue has suddenly surfaced again in the Diet, Japan's parliament.* Exception: the Supreme Soviet, which is used on all references but should be described on first reference: *the Supreme Soviet, principal legislative body of the Soviet Union.*

foreign names

See SPELLING and CAPITALIZATION, 8h. See also RUSSIAN NAMES; ARABIC WORDS AND NAMES; SPANISH AND HISPANIC NAMES; VIETNAMESE NAMES; CHINESE WORDS AND NAMES; ACCENT MARKS.

foreign words

The use of foreign words should generally be avoided. Use the English equivalent: *Walpurgis Night,* not *Walpurgisnacht; literature,* not *belles-lettres.* If it is necessary to use foreign words, be sure they are spelled correctly, then italicize them.

Some foreign words require accent marks. See ACCENT MARKS.

Foreign words that the dictionary recognizes as English are not italicized: panzer, chaise longue, kamikaze, à la carte, burrito, habeas corpus, kulak, pasta. Words that are italicized in Webster's New World Dictionary, third edition, are italicized in text: *glasnost, Luftwaffe, tummler.* Exceptions: angst,* Beaux-Arts,* couturier,* en route.*

In recipes and other articles about food, and in any article in which a foreign word is used repeatedly, such as *glasnost,* it is italicized only on first reference, to avoid creating a typographical muddle. For the same reason, it is not italicized in headlines (or set in Roman type in italic headlines).

See also ACCENT MARKS.

former, retired

Do not capitalize or abbreviate nonmilitary titles preceded by *former* or *retired*: *former president Jimmy Carter, former representative Barbara Jordan, retired professor Andrew Smith.* The reason is that once the person leaves the office or position, he or she no longer has the title. The word becomes merely descriptive, so it is not abbreviated. Do not use *former* or *retired* when referring to something done while the person was in office: *In 1980 President Jimmy Carter imposed a grain embargo,* not *In 1980 former president Jimmy Carter imposed a grain embargo.* The construction *then-* should be avoided as clumsy, but when used takes the normal capitalized title: *then-Chief Justice Earl Warren, then-Rep. Sam Jones (R-Utah).*

Fort

Do not abbreviate, except in headlines.

fortuitous

It means happening by chance, accidental. It is not a synonym for *fortunate. Their meeting at the airport was entirely fortuitous. It was fortunate that he was alone at the time.*

Frankenstein

In the novel by Mary Wollstonecraft Shelley, Frankenstein was the name of the medical student who created a monster that destroyed him. It was not the name of the monster. It misuses the cliche to say *He created a Frankenstein.*

fraternal organizations

The names of fraternal organizations, clubs etc. and their members are capitalized: *the Knights of Columbus, a Knight of Columbus; the Boy Scouts of America, a Boy Scout; the Shrine, a Shriner; the Odd Fellows, an Odd Fellow; the Benevolent and Protective Order of Elks, an Elk.*

free

It means for nothing: *Get out of jail free. They gave the apples away free* is itself redundant. *They gave the apples away for free* is doubly redundant. Similarly, *free gift* is redundant.

freelance (noun, verb and adjective)

Freestate Raceway

French

Following the style of Webster's New World Dictionary, capitalize French as an adjective even when it is not actually referring to France: *French toast, French cuffs, French doors* etc. The exception is *french fries.*

*french fries**

freshman

A first-year student in college or high school is a freshman, male or female. See also SEXISM AND SEX-BASED LANGUAGE.

Frisbee

This is the rare case in which the trade name is also the generic name, for the disk and the game. It should be capitalized. See also TRADE NAMES.

fulfill, fulfillment

full-court press

fund-raising (noun and adjective); **fund-raiser**

Gadhafi, Moammar
Ruler of Libya. The name is sometimes spelled differently by other news organizations; library references should be checked under Qaddafi, Khazaffi and Kaddafi. See also ARABIC WORDS AND NAMES.

gauntlet, gantlet
A *gauntlet* is a glove. A *gantlet* was a military punishment in which the victim ran between two lines of soldiers who beat him. In the cliches, you *throw down the gauntlet*, you *run the gantlet*.

gay
See HOMOSEXUAL.

gender
Gender is a grammatical term, not a physiological one. A noun is masculine, feminine or neuter in gender. A person is of the male or female sex. *Gender* should not be used as a synonym or euphemism for sex except in a few common expressions that have crept into the language such as *gender gap* and *gender-specific*.

geographic names
The first reference source for all geographic names not listed in this book is the National Geographic Atlas of the World. Many place names are listed in Webster's New World Dictionary, but in the few cases where the dictionary conflicts with the atlas, the atlas prevails: *Hercegovina*, not *Herzegovina*. Note, however, that in some parts of the world, including the Middle East and the Soviet Union, the atlas uses literal transliterations of local names, adding the conventional western spelling only for places that are well known:

Makkah (Mecca); Dimashq (Damascus); Moskva (Moscow). Where the conventional name is given, use it. There is no firm rule on the spelling of those places for which no common English equivalent is given. Consult the gazetteer in the newsroom computer system for guidance. See also ARABIC WORDS AND NAMES; CHINESE WORDS AND NAMES; VIETNAMESE NAMES; ACCENT MARKS.

Georgetown University Law Center
Official name of the law school. *Georgetown University Law School* is acceptable.

gibe, jibe
To *gibe* is to sneer. *Jibe* is a sailing term, meaning the movement of the boom from one side of a vessel to another when the wind is from the stern. Colloquially, it means to mesh, to be in agreement: *His words don't jibe with his actions.*

goal line (noun and adjective); *goal post*
goalkeeper, goaltender, goaltending

golf clubs
Designations are hyphenated. *3-wood, 5-iron.*

gourmet, gourmand
A *gourmet* is a connoisseur of food. A *gourmand* is a hearty eater. In general, gourmet should not be used as an adjective because a gourmet is a person, not a type of food or type of restaurant. Try to use a more precise expression: sumptuous meal, lavish dinner, expensive restaurant etc.

governor
Abbreviate as a political title: *Gov. Joan Smith of Utah.* Do not abbreviate for a member of the Federal Reserve Board: *Fed Governor John Brown.* See also TITLES and ABBREVIATIONS.

graduate

A college graduates a class. A student graduates from a college. *Dartmouth College graduated its 200th class last year. He graduated from Columbia in 1985.*

graffiti

This is a plural noun and requires a plural verb. *The graffiti were obscene. Graffiti are no longer a problem in the subway.* The singular, rarely used, is *graffito.*

grisly, grizzly

Grisly means gruesome. A *grizzly* is a bear.

gross national product

Lowercase, but the abbreviation is GNP.

Hains Point

This is the spit of land jutting into the Potomac River that contains East Potomac Park. When referring to the tennis courts, golf course etc. and the U.S. Park Police headquarters, use *East Potomac Park,* not *Hains Point.*

half-mast, half-staff

Flags fly at half-staff unless they are on ships or at naval installations on shore, where they fly at half-mast.

halftime*

handicapped

See DISABLED.

handoff (noun); hand off (verb)

hanged, hung

A person is *hanged*. Pictures and Christmas stockings are *hung*.

Hanukah

Harpers Ferry (W.Va.)

headlines

Headlines should convey as much information as possible and should capture the most important element of a story. In general:

a. It is not always necessary to have a verb. Once in a while a headline such as *The Redskins' Darkest Hour* will convey the idea of a story without a verb. If there is a verb, the subject must be stated. Do not use headlines such as *Calls Mayor Crackpot* or *Slay 6 in Drug Raid*.

b. Headlines are in the present or future tense unless a specific time element in the past is mentioned or understood.

Consumer Spending Increases
Consumer Spending Increased in July

Three Gunmen Assassinate President
Three Gunmen Assassinated Kennedy

c. Auxiliary verbs and forms of the verb *to be* may usually be omitted, but they are required in the progressive and after *says*:

ACCEPTABLE:

Budget Deficit Intolerable, Candidate Says
Candidate Calls Budget Deficit Intolerable
Driver Held Blameless in Beltway Crash

UNACCEPTABLE:

Candidate Says Budget Deficit Intolerable
Budget Deficit Said Intolerable
Driver Said Blameless in Beltway Crash

ACCEPTABLE:

Farmers Fear River Is Rising
Farmers Fear Rising River
Israelis Feared PLO Was Infiltrating

UNACCEPTABLE:

Farmers Fear River Rising
Israelis Feared PLO Infiltrating

d. The verb must be used in an independent clause following a conjunction.

ACCEPTABLE:

SE Mother Charged After Girl
Is Found Stabbed, Wandering

UNACCEPTABLE:

SE Mother Charged After Girl
Found Stabbed, Wandering

The latter construction, which appeared in the paper, makes it seem as if *girl* is the object of the *charged after* and *found* is a participle. To avoid this kind of awkwardness and confusion, the independent clause must have a verb.

e. Headlines built around puns, jokes and rhymes are rarely appropriate on news stories but are sometimes appropriate on feature stories. When in doubt about whether such a headline is appropriate, don't use it. If a headline contains a pun, all possible meanings of the play on words should be appropriate to the story.

f. Use the active voice as much as possible in preference to the passive voice.

g. A jump headline should contain some theme or key word that is the same as in the front-page headline. A headline that appears totally unrelated to the front-page headline confuses the reader, especially if more than one story jumps to the same page. If, for example, the front-page headline says *Prices, Interest Rates Rose in April* the jump headline should not say *President Renews Pledge on Taxes*, even if the second half of the story stresses this second idea. When a story inside the paper jumps to a facing page, however, unrelated themes and words may be used in the jump headline because the continuity is apparent.

h. Do not repeat words in a headline, bank or poster.

i. The strictures of headline formats sometimes make it necessary to end a line of a headline with an adjective separated from its noun or with a preposition or conjunction. This is permissible so long as the headline that results is clear and unambiguous.

j. Abbreviations that use upper- and lowercase together, such as Pr. William, Md. and Va. are typographically unattractive but may be used when there is no alternative. See also CAPITALIZATION; ABBREVIATIONS; NUMERALS.

heart failure

This should not be given as a cause of death. Every death involves heart failure. Be specific. A person dies of heart disease, or after a heart attack. See also "The Craft of the Obituary," Chapter 4.

Hechinger
See DEPARTMENT STORES.

Hecht Co., the
See DEPARTMENT STORES.

Hispanic
See RACE AND RACIAL INDENTIFICATION.

Hispanic names
See SPANISH AND HISPANIC NAMES.

historic, historical
Historic means history-making: *a historic event. Historical* means pertaining to history: *historical research.*

hit-and-run (adjective)

hoard, horde
To *hoard* is to save. That which is saved is a hoard. A *horde* is a multitude, usually of people.

hoi polloi
Not *the hoi polloi. Hoi polloi* is Greek for *the many*, meaning the common people. *Hoi* means *the*, so *the hoi polloi* is redundant.

holocaust
A *holocaust* is a fire that kills many people, not just any bad fire. Capitalize *the Holocaust,* the systematic destruction of Europe's Jews by the Nazis.

*home town** (noun); *hometown* (adjective)

homogenous, homogeneous

Homogenous means similar in structure because of common descent. *Homogeneous* is generally used to mean composed of similar or identical elements or parts. *Sweden has a homogeneous population.*

homosexual, gay

A person's sexual orientation should not be mentioned unless relevant to the story. When it is necessary to mention it, *gay* may be used as an adjective but not as a noun: *gay man, gay woman.* In headlines, *gays* may be used in the plural. A gay woman may be referred to as a lesbian. Do not use *gays and lesbians*; the first includes the second. Use *gay-rights activist*, not *gay activist.* Not everyone espousing gay-rights causes is homosexual. When identifying an individual as gay or homosexual, be cautious about invading the privacy of someone who may not wish his or her sexual preference known. Do not use terms such as *avowed* or *admitted.*

Horatio Alger

See ALGER, HORATIO.

house, home

A *house* is a structure. A *home* is a place where someone lives. Contractors build houses, not homes. Real estate agents sell houses, not homes. *His company builds houses that sell for $1 million or more. She sold her house and moved to her son's home in Arizona.* Do not use *townhome.* See also LUXURY.

hyphen

Hyphens are used in most compound words and with many prefixes and suffixes. The general rule is to hyphenate compounds, prefixes and suffixes when they are hyphenated in Webster's New World Dictionary and when necessary for clarity. See COMPOUND WORDS;

PREFIXES; SUFFIXES. In addition:

a. Use hyphens to indicate joint relationships and dual roles: *city-county cooperation; comedy-drama; writer-director John Smith.*

b. In titles, use a hyphen only to indicate a combined office or non-incumbency: *vice president;* secretary general; editor in chief; secretary-treasurer; president-elect.*

c. Hyphenate the names of weapons and aircraft where the hyphen is included in the official nomenclature. See WEAPONS AND WEAPONS SYSTEMS and AIRCRAFT.

d. Use a hyphen between a single capital letter and a noun, participle or number: *H-bomb; the A-list; V-necked; T-shirt; I-95; B-1 bomber.*

e. Some phrases of three or more words are joined by hyphens. Hyphenate those that are hyphenated in the dictionary and those including *to be: ladies-in-waiting; father-to-be.*

f. Hyphenate when spelling out numbers containing two elements: *twenty-five; three-quarters; half-dozen.*

g. Hyphenate between sets of figures and between figures and nouns in modifiers: *a 6-4 guard; 4-1 odds; 20-20 vision; a 5-6, 125-pound woman; a 12-ounce glass; a 2-by-4; a two-vote margin; a 21-7 victory; the 1986-87 season* (but *He coached at Maryland from 1983 to 1987*, not *from 1983-87*). Omit the hyphen between figures when the word *to* is used: *a 5 to 4 ruling, a vote of 326 to 97*. Only sports scores omit the *to*. See NUMERALS. See also DIMENSIONS.

h. Hyphenate an adjectival phrase that is used as a noun or to which a noun ending has been added: *a class of 6-year-olds; a sixth-grader; a supply-sider.*

i. For style on vote totals, sports scores, weights and measures etc., see NUMERALS. See also DIMENSIONS.

if and when

A meaningless redundancy. Omit *and when*.

if not more
When coupled with such expressions as *up to* or *as much as*, this renders a sentence meaningless. *The project could cost as much as $5 million if not more* conveys no information about the cost. It could be $5 million, or more, or less. If the maximum is known, use it. If not, say so, and say why. See UP TO . . . OR MORE.

illegal alien
See UNDOCUMENTED.

illegitimate
This word should not be used in referring to a person whose parents were not married. If it is necessary to raise the matter at all, use an expression such as *whose mother was not married, whose parents were not married* or *was born to an unmarried teenager.*

Immaculate Conception
The term is often misused. It refers to the conception of Mary, not the conception of Jesus. In the Roman Catholic religion, the doctrine of the Immaculate Conception holds that Mary, uniquely among human beings, was from the moment of her conception free from the stain of original sin upon her soul—a spiritual condition that made her suitable to become the mother of Jesus. The Immaculate Conception should not be confused with the virgin birth, which refers to the conception of Jesus.

imply, infer
To *imply* is to convey an idea without stating it specifically. To *infer* is the opposite: to conclude or deduce an idea that has not been specifically stated. *He inferred from the boss's kind words that he would be getting a raise, but the boss didn't mean to imply that.*

impostor

inauguration, inaugural

The event or ceremony is the *inauguration*, a noun. The adjective is *inaugural*. Capitalize *Inauguration Day*, referring to a presidential inauguration. Capitalize *inaugural* only as part of a proper name. *They went to one of the inaugural balls. They ignored his inaugural address. She organized the official White House Inaugural Ball.* Also capitalize *John F. Kennedy's Inaugural Address*, a speech that acquired a historic character. See also CAPITALIZATION.

include

It means to list some elements but not all. When all elements are given, the word include should not be used. If a presidential candidate carries six states, for example, it is correct to say: *The states he carried included A, B and C.* But if you name them all say: *The states he carried were A, B, C, D, E and F.*

Indian

The generic word for the indigenous people of the Western Hemisphere, their tribes and cultures is *Indian*. Use *Native American* in references to specific groups or organizations that have adopted the term.

indictment

An indictment is a formal charge accusing a person or an organization of committing a felony, issued after a grand jury has decided there is a valid case. An indictment is handed up or returned by the grand jury, not handed down. Issuance of an indictment may precede or follow the arrest of the suspect.

informant, informer

An informant is a source of information. An informer is one who provides evidence or accusatory information, usually for money. The police often try to fudge this distinction precisely because of the unsavory connotations of *informer*, but the newspaper should be clear about it.

innocent, not guilty

In court proceedings, there is no plea or verdict of innocent. Use *not guilty*: *He pleaded not guilty. The jury found her not guilty.*

Note that in civil proceedings, as opposed to criminal prosecutions, there is no verdict of guilty or not guilty. A jury may find a defendant responsible or liable for damages, but not guilty. Avoid constructions such as *The jury found the doctor guilty of malpractice.*

inter-

See PREFIXES.

intersection

Often unnecessary. In a sentence such as *The accident occurred at the intersection of Ninth and Main streets*, there is no need for the words *the intersection of.* They should be omitted.

interstate highways

Route designations are spelled out on first reference, then abbreviated: *Interstate 66, I-66.*

intra-

See PREFIXES.

irregardless

This is not a word in standard English. Use *regardless.*

Ivy League

The Ivy League is a formal organization of eight colleges and universities that have adopted similar academic standards and athletic policies. The schools are Brown, Columbia, Cornell, Dartmouth,

Harvard, Pennsylvania, Princeton and Yale. As an adjective, *Ivy League* may be used informally to describe the fashions, habits or political views associated with those schools and other selective schools in the Northeast, but the term is imprecise at best.

Jeep
See TRADE NAMES AND BRANDS.

Johns Hopkins University; Johns Hopkins Hospital

Joint Chiefs of Staff
Capitalize and use a plural verb. *The Joint Chiefs of Staff are unhappy with the policy.* Capitalize *Joint Chiefs* on second reference.

judges and judicial titles
See COURTS AND LEGAL TERMINOLOGY.

jump shot

jurist
A jurist is a scholar of the law. Not every judge is a jurist and the words should not be used synonymously.

juveniles
Juveniles are persons under the age of 18. Juveniles who are arrested or accused by the police of committing crimes are not identified by name unless a judge or magistrate has ordered that they be tried as adults.

On second reference, there is no clear demarcation between those who are referred to by last name only, like adults, and those referred to by first name, like children. In general, use the last name for juveniles 16 and over, first name for those under 16. Exceptions may be warranted in the case of juveniles charged as adults in court cases (in which case the defendant may be named) or juvenile athletes or performers.

K mart Corp.; K mart stores

Kalashnikov
Soviet arms manufacturer. Its best-known product is the AK-47 assault rifle, also manufactured in many other countries.

Kennedy Center
The formal name is the *John F. Kennedy Center for the Performing Arts*; informally, *the Kennedy Center.* When writing about a particular performance, specify the hall: *Opera House, Eisenhower Theater* etc.

kickoff (noun); kick off (verb)

kidnap (verb); kidnapped, kidnapping, kidnapper

kids
This is not used as a generic synonym for *children* or *youths*, even in headlines.

King, Martin Luther, Jr.
The federal holiday is Martin Luther King Jr. Day (not birthday). It honors the Rev. Martin Luther King Jr. Use *Dr.* only in quotations. Do not use *the late* with the name of Martin Luther King Jr.

Kings Dominion (Va.)

knot
A nautical knot is a measurement of speed: 6,076.1 feet an hour, or 1.15 mph. A ship sails at 10 knots, not 10 knots an hour.

Korean names
Some Koreans put family names first (*Kim Il Sung, Kim*) and some put them last (*Tongsun Park, Park*). In either case, no hyphens are used.

kudos
This is a Greek noun meaning praise or glory. It is not a plural. There is no such thing as a *kudo*. The word is trite and best avoided. Use praise or honors.

La Guardia Airport (New York)

Ladies Professional Golf Association
Abbreviated *LPGA*. In sports stories only, *LPGA* is acceptable on first reference.

Lafayette Square
Not *Lafayette Park*, except in quotations. Historians and cartographers differ about this, but the District of Columbia government's official street map shows *Lafayette Square*.

laissez faire (noun); laissez-faire (adjective)
The dictionary lists these as English words. They are not italicized.

lame duck (noun); lame-duck (adjective)
A lame duck is an elected official who, not having been reelected, is serving out the last post-election weeks of his term. Ronald Reagan became a lame duck when his successor was elected in November 1988. An elected official who is barred by law from running for an additional term should not be described as a lame duck until a successor has been chosen. The governor of Virginia, for example, is limited by law to a single term, but is hardly a lame duck on the day of inauguration.

late, the late

There is no firm rule on how long someone must be dead before he or she is no longer referred to as *the late*. Historic personages and famous people whose deaths are well known—John F. Kennedy, Duke Ellington, Earl Warren, Martin Luther King Jr., Marilyn Monroe—should never be referred to as *the late*. Also, the expression should never be used to describe actions the person took while alive. Do not say *He served in the Cabinet of the late president Lyndon B. Johnson* or *The late John Cheever wrote the book*. He was not dead at the time. If his death must be mentioned, rephrase: *John Cheever wrote the book two years before his death. John Cheever, who died in 1986, wrote the book in 1984.*

Laurel Race Course

lawsuits

See COURTS AND LEGAL TERMINOLOGY, item s. See also INNOCENT, NOT GUILTY.

lawyer

See ATTORNEY.

leave, let

The words have quite different meanings when followed by *alone*. To *let alone* is to stop bothering: *Please let us alone*. To *leave alone* is to leave in solitude: *Please leave us alone for a few minutes*.

lectern

See PODIUM.

left-handed, left-hander

lend, loan

In general, use *lend* as a verb, *loan* as a noun. *The bank lent him the money. The bank refused to give her a loan.*

less, fewer

Use *fewer* when referring to the number of individuals or items, *less* when referring to the bulk or quantity. *We had fewer than 10 applicants for that job. Less than 45 seconds was left in the game. The cost was less than $1 million.* Use less with a smaller quantity (*less than a pound of sugar*), fewer with a smaller number (*fewer than 20 people*). The difficulty arises when quantity is expressed as number: $3, 15 seconds. Although 3 and 15 are numbers, the usage expresses one quantity, not counted units of money or time. In these cases, use *less*: *She had less than $3 in her purse. Less than 15 seconds remained when he kicked the field goal.*

like, as

In the perpetual confusion over when to use *like* and when to use *as*, these suggestions may be helpful:

a. Do not use *like* as a conjunction, except in direct quotation. That is, *like* should not be followed by a verb. *Food prices will rise as* (not *like*) *oil prices did. He's going to work in the mines, just as* (not *like*) *his father did. She always studied hard, just as her father taught her.*

b. As prepositions connoting comparison, use *like* to suggest resemblance or contrast, *as* to indicate degree or correlation. *She's just like her mother. There's no place like home. They were treated like royalty. He's fit as a fiddle. The movie was as dull as dishwater.*

c. Note the subtle distinction between *He was dressed like a farmer* (i.e., wearing clothing that a farmer would wear) and *He was dressed as a farmer* (i.e., wearing a costume).

linage, lineage

Linage (two syllables) is a measure of space, the number of lines taken up by an article or advertisement. *Lineage* (three syllables) means ancestry.

lion's share

This is a cliché and best avoided because it doesn't mean what many people think it means. The lion's share, according to Aesop, was the entire kill. The phrase should not be used to mean a majority or most.

litany

A litany is a form of prayer in which priest and congregation recite alternately, the congreation repeatedly giving the same response. A litany need not be doleful; it may be joyous. The word *litany* should not be used as a synonym for catalogue, complaint or list of complaints.

litmus test

A litmus test is a chemical procedure that uses litmus paper to test for acid in a solution. Most tests—of character, knowledge, staying power, ideological purity, virtue etc.—are not litmus tests. Use the metaphor only in those situations where a single visible reaction is a clear determinant of the conclusion. Avoid such sentences as *The game will be a litmus test for Maryland's pass defense.*

loan

See LEND.

loath, loathe

Loath is an adjective meaning reluctant. *Loathe* is a verb meaning detest.

located, located at

In descriptions of place, the words *located* and *located at* are often superfluous: *The warehouse where the shooting took place is located at Fifth Street and Rhode Island Avenue NE* (omit *located*). *Where is it located at?* (omit *located at*).

luxury

Careful writers avoid using this as an adjective. Use *luxurious* if something truly is elegant or sumptuous; otherwise, use *expensive, lavish, elegant* or some other precise term. An empty apartment cannot be luxurious. The "luxury homes" advertised in the paper are more accurately described as expensive houses. The adjective *luxuriant* means lush, as in a garden.

maitre d'

This is a colloquial abbreviation of the French *maître d'hôtel*. Generally its use should be restricted to direct quotations. In standard text, it is preferable to use the English equivalent, *headwaiter*.

major league (noun and adjective); major-leaguer

But *Major League Baseball* in references to the corporate entity.

majority

This may take a singular or plural verb, depending on context. As a collective noun meaning most of a group, it takes the plural: *He said a majority of the Democrats are against the measure.* (In such cases, however, confusion can be avoided by substituting *most* for *a majority of.*) Otherwise, it is necessary to decide whether the subject is the individuals or the group as a whole: *The majority were against the bill even before it was amended. The Republican majority is determined to shelve the measure.*

majority, plurality

A majority is more than half. A plurality is the highest number, not necessarily a majority. This is a crucial distinction in reporting election results.

man, -man

See SEXISM AND SEX-BASED LANGUAGE.

manner, manor

Manner means behavior. A *manor* is an estate. Note, however, that an aristocrat is said to be *to the manner born*—that is, heir to aristocratic behavior, not heir to the land. The expression is from "Hamlet":

> HORATIO: *Is it a custom?*
> HAMLET: *Ay, marry, is't;*
>   *But to my mind,—though I am native here,*
>   *And to the manner born,—it is a custom*
>   *More honour'd in the breach than the observance.*

mantel, mantle

A *mantel* is a shelf. A *mantle* is a cloak.

maps

Like headlines, maps and other graphics require more flexibility in abbreviation than does text. Throughout this stylebook, where exceptions are permitted for headlines they may be taken as permitted for maps, graphics and tabular matter as well.

Marine Corps, Marines

Capitalize *Marine* and *Marines* in all references to the U.S. Marine Corps, its units and its members. *The Marines have landed. Two*

Marines were wounded. Capt. John Smith was in command of the Marine patrol.

market basket*

marshal, martial

A *marshal* is a law enforcement officer or military commander, as in *field marshal*. *Martial* means pertaining to war—from the Latin possessive form of Mars, the god of war. Hence *martial law, court-martial*.

matzoh*

May Day, Mayday

May Day, or May 1, is the occasion for spring festivals and the international labor holiday. *Mayday* is a distress signal.

Mazza Gallerie

The shopping center on Wisconsin Avenue NW.

Mecca, mecca

Mecca, in Saudi Arabia, is the holiest city in Islam, birthplace of Muhammad and site of a shrine all Moslems are obliged to visit. Lowercase, *mecca*, is a metaphorical term for a place many people desire to visit. Do not use it in association with illegal or nefarious activities. Avoid such expressions as *a mecca for drug dealers*.

Medal of Honor

The nation's highest military decoration. Not Congressional Medal of Honor.

media

The noun *medium* has two plural forms. *Mediums* are spiritualists. *Media* are methods or means, as in media of communications. As a plural noun, *media* takes a plural verb, except in direct quotation. *The media are biased. She said the media were taking control of the campaign.*

median
See AVERAGE.

Metro
See WASHINGTON METROPOLITAN AREA TRANSIT AUTHORITY.

Metropolitan Washington Council of Governments
Abbreviated *COG* on subsequent reference.

middle age (noun); middle-aged (adjective)
See also AGE.

midshipman
Every student at the U.S. Naval Academy, male or female, is a *midshipman*. Students at the Naval Academy are not cadets.

MiG
Soviet aircraft. The name is an acronym formed from the names of its designers, Mikoyan and Gurevich. It takes a hyphen with a numerical designation: *MiG-21.*

military ranks and titles
All members of the U.S. armed forces fall into one of three groups: officers, warrant officers and enlisted personnel. Enlisted personnel, with the ranks of sergeant or petty officer and below, are never referred to as officers.

The commander in chief of the armed forces is the president. The nation's senior military officer is the chairman of the Joint Chiefs of Staff. The senior officers of the Army and the Air Force are the chiefs of staff of those services. The senior Navy officer is the chief of naval operations. The senior officer of the Marine Corps is the commandant.

Students at the U.S. Naval Academy are midshipmen.

Students at the U.S. Military Academy and the Air Force Academy are cadets.

As with other titles, military ranks and titles are capitalized when placed before the name of an individual, lowercase when standing alone: *Maj. Gen. William Brown. He was promoted to major general.*

Here are the military ranks and the abbreviations used as titles before names. They are listed in descending order. Note that designations of rank ending in -man, such as airman and seaman, apply to men and women.

ARMY

Commissioned Officers

Rank	Abbreviation
general	Gen.
lieutenant general	Lt. Gen.
major general	Maj. Gen.
brigadier general	Brig. Gen.
colonel	Col.
lieutenant colonel	Lt. Col.
major	Maj.
captain	Capt.
first lieutenant	1st Lt.
second lieutenant	2nd Lt.

Warrant Officers

Rank	Abbreviation
chief warrant officer	not abbreviated
warrant officer	not abbreviated

Enlisted Personnel

Rank	Abbreviation
sergeant major of the Army	Army Sgt. Maj.
command sergeant major	Command Sgt. Maj.
staff sergeant major	Staff Sgt. Maj.
first sergeant	1st Sgt.
master sergeant	Master Sgt.
platoon sergeant	Platoon Sgt.
sergeant first class	Sgt. 1st Class
specialist seven	Spec. 7
staff sergeant	Staff Sgt.
specialist six	Spec. 6
sergeant	Sgt.
specialist five	Spec. 5
corporal	Cpl.
specialist four	Spec. 4
private first class	Pfc.
private 2, private 1	Pvt.

AIR FORCE

Commissioned Officers

Ranks and abbreviations for commissioned officer are the same as in the Army.

Enlisted Personnel

Rank	Abbreviation
chief master sergeant of the Air Force	Chief Master Sgt.
senior master sergeant	Senior Master Sgt.
master sergeant	Master Sgt.

Rank	Abbreviation
technical sergeant	Tech. Sgt.
staff sergeant	Staff Sgt.
sergeant	Sgt.
airman first class	Airman 1st Class
airman, airman basic	Airman

NAVY, COAST GUARD

Commissioned Officers

Rank	Abbreviation
admiral	Adm.
vice admiral	Vice Adm.
rear admiral upper half	Rear Adm.
rear admiral lower half	Rear Adm.
captain	Capt.
commander	Cmdr.
lieutenant commander	Lt. Cmdr.
lieutenant	Lt.
lieutenant junior grade	Lt. j.g.
ensign	Ensign

Warrant Officers

Rank	Abbreviation
chief warrant officer	not abbreviated
warrant officer	not abbreviated

Enlisted Personnel

Rank	Abbreviation
master chief petty officer	Master Chief Petty Officer
senior chief petty officer	Senior Chief Petty Officer
chief petty officer	Chief Petty Officer
petty officer first class	Petty Officer 1st Class
petty officer second class	Petty Officer 2nd Class
petty officer third class	Petty Officer 3rd Class
seaman	Seaman
seaman apprentice	Seaman Apprentice
seaman recruit	Seaman Recruit

MARINE CORPS

Ranks and abbreviations for commissioned officers are the same as in the Army. Warrant officer ratings follow the Navy system. There are no specialist ratings.

Enlisted Personnel

Rank	Abbreviation
sergeant major	Sgt. Maj.
master gunnery sergeant	Master Gunnery Sgt.
master sergeant	Master Sgt.
first sergeant	1st Sgt.
gunnery sergeant	Gunnery Sgt.
staff sergeant	Staff Sgt.
sergeant	Sgt.
corporal	Cpl.
lance corporal	Lance Cpl.
private first class	Pfc.
private	Pvt.

For style on retired officers, see TITLES, item i.

millimeter

In weapons and other measurements, abbreviate and run together with numerals: *a 9mm pistol, a 35mm camera.*

million

Spell out the word when using it as a general term of abundance: *He helped this team a million ways.* Use 1 million for the specific number: *The budget was $1 million; a $1 million budget.* See also NUMERALS.

minuscule, not miniscule

mishap

A *mishap* is an unfortunate accident. The word conveys the idea that the accident is not serious. A plane crash that kills 200 people may be a disaster or a tragedy, but not a mishap.

molotov cocktail*

Moslem, Muslim

Adherents of the religion of Islam throughout the world are Moslems. They prefer to be called Muslims, but in the United States the word *Muslim* has been taken over by the group known as Nation of Islam, headed by Louis Farrakhan. Farrakhan's followers call themselves Muslims but their beliefs and practices differ in many ways from those of Islam. The easiest way to preserve this distinction is to use *Moslems* in all references except to members of the Nation of Islam, who are Muslims. Do not use the term *Black Muslim.* Note that most Moslems throughout the world are not Arabs. Do not equate Islam or Moslems with the Arab world. Nearly all Iranians, for example, are Moslems but they are not Arabs. See also RELIGION AND THE CLERGY and AYATOLLAH.

Mount

Do not abbreviate, except in headlines.

Mr., Mrs., Miss, Ms.

Men and women alike are generally referred to by surname only on second reference. Rep. Louis Brown is Brown. George Williams is Williams. Col. Andrew White is White. Karen Smith is Smith. Lucy Price-Jackson is Price-Jackson. Sister Mary Agnes O'Brien is O'Brien if she uses her last name. Otherwise, Sister Mary Agnes on second reference.

Mr., Mrs. etc. are used on second reference in obituaries, in references to couples, for spouses of heads of state and of other prominent individuals, in quotations and where necessary for effect, as in editorials and critiques. *He sued Mr. and Mrs. Black. Mr. Black owes the voters an explanation. "Ms. Black is out of step with the voters," he said. While the chancellor was addressing Congress, Mrs. Kohl had tea with the First Lady. She called herself Ms. Johnson.*

Married women are referred to by their first names and surnames, without *Mrs.*, unless only the husband's first name is known: *Helen Black* (not Mrs. John Black). *Police identified the victims as Mr. and Mrs. John Black. They said Mrs. Black was not wearing a seat belt.*

See also TITLES.

Muhammad, Mohammed

See ARABIC WORDS AND NAMES.

music

a.   The names of popular, jazz, folk, rock and country compositions and songs are capitalized and put in quotation marks. *The orchestra played "Begin the Beguine" but she wanted to hear "Stardust." He remembered "Lucy in the Sky with Diamonds" but he forgot "Yesterday." Paul Desmond was the saxophonist on Brubeck's "Take Five" album.*

b. Classical compositions are often identified by at least two
    types of generic information—genre, key, instrumenta-
    tion and number in a series of the same genre—along
    with a coined name. In titles of classical works, capitalize
    all generic elements of the title. Capitalize the coined
    name and put it in quotes. Consult the Schwann record,
    tape and compact disc guides for titles of classical works.
    Examples:

    Beethoven's Symphony No. 5 in C Minor, Op. 67
    Beethoven's Symphony No. 3 in E-flat ("Eroica")
    Beethoven's Third Symphony
    Beethoven's Symphonies Nos. 3 and 4
    Tchaikovsky's "Nutcracker" Suite
    Tchaikovsky's ballet "The Nutcracker"
    Dvorak's Symphony No. 9 in E Minor, the "New World"
        symphony
    Prokofiev's "Alexander Nevsky"

c. In informal usage when referring to a symphony by a very
    well-known composer, the word *symphony* may be omitted:
    Beethoven's Ninth, Brahms's Third. General references are
    lowercase: *The orchestra played a Mozart symphony and two
    overtures by Puccini.*

d. When a concerto is a work for solo instrument with or-
    chestra, as is usually the case, the form *Piano Concerto,
    Horn Concerto* etc. may be used instead of *Concerto for Piano
    and Orchestra* etc. But *a concerto for violin and piano*, not *a
    violin and piano concerto. Bartok's Concerto for Orchestra.*

e. When giving key signatures, specify *minor* but not *major.*
    Capitalize *minor* as part of a title but lowercase in general
    references: *Symphony in C, his Concerto in E Minor, a minor*

chord. Use the forms *E-flat, F-sharp* etc. in all references, including titles.

f.   Use English titles for classical compositions and operas unless the Schwann catalogue specifies otherwise. Languages other than English are in quotation marks. *Ravel's Violin Sonata, Berlioz's "Symphonie Fantastique," Beethoven's "Missa Solemnis."* In referring to a particular opera production, use the language the opera company is using: *Mozart's "The Marriage of Figaro," the Metropolitan Opera's "Le Nozze di Figaro."* In English titles, the words *Mass* and *Requiem* are capitalized: *Haydn's "Mass in Time of War," Verdi's Requiem.*

g.   Follow Webster's New World Dictionary for plurals of musical terms: *tempos, concertos.*

h.   Abbreviate references to publishers' opus numbers and to catalogue listings of a composer's work: *Vivaldi's "The Four Seasons," Op. 8, Nos. 1–4. Mozart's Symphony No. 40, K. 550.* (K. is the abbreviation for the Koechel catalogue of Mozart's works.)

i.   Use *piano* and *cello* in all references, not *pianoforte* or *violoncello.*

j.   Titles of arias are lowercase except for the first word: *"Un bel di," "O sole mio."*

k.   In some contemporary pieces, the "genre" is actually a coined name. These are subject to the editor's judgment. When in doubt, use quotation marks. *William Smith's "Fancies" for Clarinet.*

l.   Capitalize the names of sections of a piece of classical music that are labeled by tempo: *The Allegro con Brio movement; the Adagio section.*

m. Lowercase musical styles and periods except for Renaissance: *baroque, romantic.* See also CAPITALIZATION. The word *classical* is capitalized when necessary to distinguish the Classical period (c. 1750–1825) from classical music in general.

Nation of Islam
See MOSLEM, MUSLIM.

National Basketball Association
Abbreviated as NBA. In sports stories only, NBA is acceptable on first reference.

National Building Museum
This landmark structure on Judiciary Square was formerly known as the Pension Building. It was officially renamed by act of Congress in 1980.

National Collegiate Athletic Association
Abbreviated as NCAA, which is always acceptable on first reference.

National Football League
Abbreviated as NFL. In sports stories, NFL is acceptable on first reference. The players' union is the NFL Players Association on all references.

National Governors' Association
Do not abbreviate.

National Guard
Unless nationalized by the president, National Guard units are state organizations. Specify the state: *the Minnesota National Guard, the Alabama Air National Guard.* On second reference, *the National Guard, the Guard; a National Guardsman, a guardsman.*

National Hockey League
Abbreviated as NHL. In sports stories, NHL is acceptable on first reference.

National Institutes of Health
This is the collective name for institutes that form the biomedical research arm of the federal government. All are in Bethesda. On second reference, *NIH*, not *the NIH*. When writing about individual scientists or specific research projects, specify the institute: the National Heart, Lung and Blood Institute, the National Cancer Institute etc.

National Organization for Women
Not the National Organization of Women. The acronym is *NOW*.

Native American
See INDIAN.

New York
The name of the city is New York. It is called New York City only when necessary to distinguish it from the rest of the state.

nicknames
When nicknames are used, they are in quotation marks, not parentheses. *Clarence "Frogman" Henry; Thomas P. "Tip" O'Neill Jr.* Nicknames are common in stories about sports and show business, but they should be used with care in crime stories. Law enforcement officials who attach nicknames such as *the Weasel* to people they are arresting are making statements the newspaper does not necessarily want to echo. Ordinary nicknames and diminutives—Ed, Bill, Joe, Pete, Tom etc.—need not be given on first reference and are not put in quotation marks when used.

nom de guerre, nom de plume

Nom de guerre is a French term meaning war name. It has no English equivalent and may be used in sentences such as *The attack was planned by the terrorist whose nom de guerre is Abu Nidal.* The plural, rarely used, is *noms de guerre. Nom de plume* means pen name. Use the English term unless there is some compelling reason to use French. *Mark Twain was the pen name of Samuel Clemens.*

non-

See PREFIXES.

none

The word may be singular or plural, depending on context: *None of the bread is fresh. None of the eggs in the nest was broken. None of the bacteria were identified.* This is true also when referring to people: *None of the players was any good. Of all the victims, none are more pitiable than the orphaned children.*

not only . . . but

This common expression must link word constructions that are parallel: *Not only* noun *but also* noun. *Not only* verb *but also* verb. *Not only* clause *but* clause. Examples:

   They not only beat the Giants but the Cowboys.

This is an incorrect construction (*not only* verb *but* noun). Make it: *They beat not only the Giants but also the Cowboys* (*not only* noun *but also* noun) or *They not only beat the Giants but thrashed the Cowboys* (*not only* verb *but* verb).

   The City Council not only adjourned but the members went on vacation.

This is incorrect (*not only* verb *but* independent clause). Make it *Not only did the City Council adjourn but the members went on vacation* (*not only* independent clause *but* independent clause).

not so much

The second half of this construction begins with *as*, not *but: It was not so much hatred of the king that inspired them as their deep commitment to democracy.*

number

This may take a singular or plural verb, depending on the context. In general, it takes a singular verb when used with the article *the* and the actual number is the subject. *The number of AIDS cases keeps growing. He said the number of defectors has grown to 208.* It takes a plural verb when used with the indefinite article *a*, and when the group is the subject. *A growing number of Americans are afflicted with AIDS. A number of the defectors are very unhappy here.*

number one, No. 1

See ABBREVIATIONS, 4c. See also NUMERALS.

numerals

In general, it is easier to understand numbers expressed in figures than in words. As a rule, spell out numbers one through nine in ordinary text. Use figures for higher numbers and for statistical and sequential forms. Apply this rule to both cardinal forms (one, two . . . 10, 11, 12) and ordinal forms (first, second . . . 10th, 11th, 12th). Use figures in all tabular matter. Roman numerals are used only sparingly.

   1. **Use figures**
       a. in addresses: *129 Stevens Ave.* Use the nine and under rule for numbered streets: *7 Ninth St. NW*; *1432 51st St.* See also ADDRESSES.

       b. in ages of people and animals: *A 4-year-old horse*; *a four-year-old building.*

c. in dates, years, and decades: *Jan. 3, 1947, class of '47, the 1940s.*

d. in centuries to enumerate specific centuries: *the 9th century, the 6th century B.C.* But spell out an adjectival use, as in *America's third century, the fifth and last century of Rome's domination.* Also spell out *Gay Nineties, Roaring Twenties.*

e. in decimals, in percentages and in fractions with numbers larger than 1: *6.5 magnitude, 3 1/2 laps, 5.25 percent interest, readings of 6.21, .02 and 0.14; 12 one-hundredths. Their sales were two-thirds, one-quarter and one-half, respectively, of what was expected.*

f. in decisions, rulings, scores and votes: *A 5 to 4 decision, ruled 6 to 3, defeated the White Sox, 5-4. They defeated the amendment by a vote of 6 to 4, by a two-vote margin.* In all such uses except sports scores, figures are separated by the word *to* and the hyphen is omitted: *A 211 to 106 vote, an 8 to 1 ruling; a 21-14 score.*

g. in dimensions and measurements containing two or more elements: *5 feet 10 inches tall, a 5-3 woman, a 9-by-12-foot rug, 2 feet by 1 foot by 8 inches.* Where there is only one element, spell out numbers less than 10: *a five-inch snowfall, four feet tall, a six-footer, a 15-mile run, an 11-hour ordeal* (but *an eleventh-hour decision*). See also RECIPES and DIMENSIONS.

h. In geographic and political districts: *Ward 3, 2nd Precinct, 8th Congressional District, 4th U.S. Circuit Court of Appeals, 3rd Police District, 4th Ward.*

i. in mathematical usage: *Multiply by 4, divide by 6. He added 2 and 2 but he got 5.*

j. in military ranks used as titles with names, military terms and weapons: *Airman 1st Class Mary Black, Petty Officer*

3rd Class John Brown, Spec. 4 Joan Williams, 1st Sgt. William Smith, M-16 rifle, 9mm pistol, 5th Division, 6th Fleet. In military ranks, spell out the figure when it is used after the name or without a name. *Smith was a second lieutenant. Everyone wants to make first sergeant. Specialists fourth class aren't admitted to the NCO Club.* See MILITARY RANKS AND TITLES.

k. in monetary units: *5 cents, $2 bill, 8 pounds, 6 pesos, $3 million.*

l. in designations of planes, ships, weapons, spacecraft and vehicles: *Apollo 8, Viking 2, B-52, M-16, Formula 2 racer, Queen Elizabeth 2* (the ship, not the monarch). An exception is *Air Force One,* the president's plane, and its backups. Use Roman numerals when part of a trade name or official designation: *Continental Mark IV.* Missile models also use Roman numerals: *Trident II.* See AIRCRAFT.

m. in odds, proportions, recipes and ratios: *a 15-1 long shot, 3 parts cement to 1 part water, 3 onions, 2 tablespoons of sugar to 1 cup of milk; a 1-in-3 chance* (but *one chance in three*).

n. in sequential designations—rooms, pages, chapters, buildings, models, sizes, positions, scenes, scales etc.: *They were out of sizes 4, 5 and 6; read Pages 8 through 23; 6 on the Richter scale; Rooms 3 and 4; Chapter 2, Act 3.* See CAPITALIZATION, 8c. In ordinal usage, spell out figures less than 10th: *He was third in his class. Her horses finished fourth and seventh.*

o. in sports scores, standings and standards. *83-78, 3 up, led 3-2, a 6-1-2 record, par 3, 5 handicap, a high jump of 6-3½.* In narrative, follow the nine-and-under rule except for yard lines in football. *The ball was on the 4-yard line, the 25-yard line. He connected on eight of 12 passes. Seventh*

hole; *three-point play*. *He went three for five*. See also GOLF
CLUBS.

p. in technical terminology: *f3.5 lens opening, 9 degrees latitude, Mach 2*.

q. in temperatures, except zero: *It was 8 degrees below zero.
The temperature dropped from 38 to 8 in two hours*. (But
temperatures in the forties, the nineties etc.)

r. in time measurements and calculations: *4 p.m., 5 o'clock,
8 hours 30 minutes 20 seconds, a winning time of 3:36.2*. But
spell out numbers less than 10 standing alone and in
modifiers. *Give me five more minutes. They scored with eight
seconds left. An eight-hour day, the two-minute warning*.

s. in a series of three or more numbers, any one of which is
larger than 10: *He had 6 goats, 8 sheep and 12 chickens. He
had six goats and 12 chickens*.

2. **Spell out**
a. at the start of a sentence: *Forty-three miners died. Forty to
50 miners are feared dead*.

b. in indefinite usage: *A hundred percent wrong; a five-and-ten-
cent store; sixty-odd, a million-dollar look; in his sixties* (as
opposed to *in the '60s*).

c. in formal language, rhetorical quotations and figures of
speech: *"Fifty-four forty or fight"; "Fourscore and seven years
ago . . . "; number one authority* (as opposed to a person or
thing that is first on an actual numbered list: *No. 1 draft
choice, ranked No. 2 in the country*. See also NUMBER ONE).
*Twelve Apostles, Ten Commandments, Gay Nineties, square one,
wouldn't touch it with a ten-foot pole, high five, Day One*.

d. in fanciful usage: *Mudville Nine, Chicago Seven*.

e. in fractions less than one that are not used as modifiers:

reduced by one-half, bigger by one-third; he threw out two-thirds of them; ½-inch pipe; ⅛-inch drill bit.

f.   with pronouns and in names of groups (unless the group itself specifies a digit): *we three; you four. The Brothers Four, the Three Sounds.*

3. Roman numerals

These are used for lineal designations of persons and animals and in proper names if so specified. Use Arabic numerals for all other lineal designations and for subdivisions of larger units: *George Wellington Cabot IV; King George III; Pope John XXIII; Native Dancer II; "The Godfather, Part II"; Continental Mark IV, Super Bowl XIV. Apollo 11.* Missiles and launch rockets also use Roman numerals. See AIRCRAFT.

4. Large numbers

a.   In referring to millions, billions and trillions, use a figure-word combination unless the number of digits is itself significant: *4 million people, a $7.4 billion budget, in the range of $50 billion to $60 billion. He proposed a budget of $1,113,057—yes, seven figures.*

b.   Multi-digit numbers should be approximated or rounded off, especially in headlines, unless the precise number is required to inform the reader: *The president requested $2.8 billion in aid. The president's aid request was $2,798,906,002.75. What do you suppose the $2.75 is for?* Two digits beyond the decimal point will usually suffice: *The painting was auctioned for $3.26 million.*

5. Punctuation of numerals

a.   In modifiers containing figures, hyphenate the compound: *eight-hour day, 10-foot board, 5-foot-6 girl.*

b. Use apostrophes for omissions but not plurals except for plurals of single letters: *class of '47*, *in the '50s* (i.e., the decade. Spell out ages and temperatures: *She was in her thirties, temperatures in the forties*); *B-52s*. *Mind your p's and q's*.

c. In spelling out numbers, use no commas. Hyphenate only after words ending in y. *One hundred seventy-five*.

d. Use commas in numbers of four or more digits but not in addresses, phone numbers, serial numbers etc.: *1,234,567 citizens*; *1234 Oak St.*; *dial 334-6000*. See also ADDRESSES and TELEPHONE NUMBERS.

obituaries
See Chapter 4.

obscene, pornographic
Obscene means offensive to prevailing notions of modesty or decency. *Pornographic* means written or filmed primarily to arouse sexual desire. Acts committed by human beings may be obscene but they are not pornographic unless filmed. See also PROFANE AND VULGAR LANGUAGE.

occur
This is not the same as *take place*. Unplanned events occur. Scheduled events take place.

off-, -off
For compound words beginning with *off-*, see PREFIXES. Compound nouns ending in *-off* may or may not take a hyphen. Follow the style in Webster's New World Dictionary: *kickoff* (noun), *kick off* (verb); *rip-off* (noun), *rip off* (verb); *sign-off* (noun), *sign off* (verb).

off-Broadway
Adjective and adverb. Always hyphenated. See BROADWAY.

Olympic Games
Olympics, the Games, the Summer Olympics, the Winter Olympics, the Summer Games, the Winter Games.

Olympic-size
An Olympic-size swimming pool is 50 meters long by 25 meters wide. A pool of any other dimensions is not Olympic-size.

ombudsman
Male or female. See SEXISM AND SEX-BASED LANGUAGE.

only
This word is often unnecessary. Omit it in sentences such as *Last year he scored 15 touchdowns but this season he has only four.* When it is used, be careful about placement. In a sentence such as *She went to the store on Saturday*, the word *only* can be placed anywhere but the placement affects the meaning. *Only she went to the store on Saturday, She went to the only store on Saturday* etc.

ophthalmologist, optometrist, optician
An *ophthalmologist* (from the Greek ophthalmos, eye) is a physician who specializes in diseases and disorders of the eye. An *optometrist* is not a physician but is a professional specialist in problems of vision and corrective lenses. An *optician* makes and sells eyeglasses and contact lenses. See also DOCTOR.

opportunist, opportunistic
An *opportunist* is one who tailors his or her beliefs or actions to circumstances in order to advance his or her interests, without regard to principle. The word should not be used to describe a person or

group that seizes opportunities presented in a morally neutral environment. If the Redskins convert five turnovers into touchdowns, they are taking advantage of opportunities, but they are not opportunists.

oral
See VERBAL.

Oriental
Do not use this adjective in reference to human beings. Use *Asian*.

out-of-
Adjectives formed from *out-of-* are hyphenated when they precede the noun: *out-of-bounds*, *out-of-pocket*, *out-of-the-way*. Omit hyphens after the noun: *The restaurant was certainly out of the way*.

over-
For compound words beginning with *over-*, see COMPOUND WORDS.

pair
It may be singular or plural. See COUPLE.

pan-
See PREFIXES for the general rule, but do not hyphenate Pan American: *Pan American World Airways*, *Pan American Union*.

parameter
A mathematical term. It means a constant of which the value varies according to the circumstances of its application. It is not a synonym for *boundary, limit* or *definition*.

parentheses and brackets
In general, parentheses ( ) may be used to indicate a writer's interpolation in his own copy. Brackets [ ] indicate material inserted

from another writer or source as well as the writer's interpolation in a quote. Both should be used sparingly because they interrupt the flow of the material.

1. **Parentheses are used to enclose**
   a. incidental comment: *He tied his dog to a tree (dogs are not allowed in the store) and went inside.*
   b. a political-geographic designation: *Sen. Paul S. Sarbanes (D-Md.).*
   c. figures or letters in a series: *The water is (a) cold, (b) muddy and (c) polluted.* This construction should be used sparingly.
   d. a specific location inserted to avoid ambiguity: *The Springfield (Ohio) News-Sun.*
   e. equivalents and translations: *It cost 2,700 lire ($1.50). They met at a remote tube (subway) stop. His party is in control of the Knesset (parliament).* But unless there is some compelling reason to retain the original word, it is better to omit it and use the translation or equivalent without parentheses. *They met at a remote subway stop. His party is in control of Israel's parliament.* See also FOREIGN LEGISLATURES.

2. **Brackets are used to enclose**
   a. explanatory material added to a quote: *"I told [Prime Minister Andrew] Black that I would be here." "I told [the committee] that we were headed for rough times."*
   b. material from another writer or service or from another dateline. Set off this material in a separate paragraph.

   [The veto is likely to have political repercussions in Illinois as well because the farm bill has been an issue in several congressional races, Washington Post special correspondent Mary Brown reported from Chicago.]

   c. later developments in a datelined story where there might be confusion about time or sequence. This material is set off in a separate paragraph.

   [*But three hours later the plane was still on the ground, the Associated Press reported.*]

   d. reference keys within a story: [*Details on Page C3.*]

Bracketed material is helpful in the interests of accuracy, but it is also distracting. Often it is better to paraphrase quotes than to load them down with bracketed material. (See QUOTATIONS.) Bracketed material and interpolated paragraphs should be grouped together rather than scattered through a story. When material from more than one external source is interpolated, it is often better to eliminate the brackets and credit all additional sources in an italicized sentence at the end of the story.

parliamentarian

In the United States, this means a person skilled in parliamentary procedure. In Britain and some other countries, it is often used to mean a member of parliament but this usage may be confusing to American readers.

Patriot Center (at George Mason University)

Not *the Patriot Center*. Omit the article.

PCB, PCP

The toxic residue polychlorinated biphenyl is abbreviated as PCB on first reference and in headlines, but should be spelled out early in a story. The psychedelic drug is PCP on all references. See AB-BREVIATIONS.

Pension Building

See NATIONAL BUILDING MUSEUM.

penultimate
It means next to last.

Peoples Drug Store
Not People's.

percent, percentage
Be careful to distinguish between percent and percentage points. In a group of 100 students, if the number taking a certain course rises from 10 to 20, enrollment in the course has risen by 100 percent, but student participation has risen by 10 percentage points. If a president's favorable rating in the polls declines from 60 percent to 40 percent, it has declined by 20 percentage points but 33⅓ percent. If interest rates rise from 8 percent to 10 percent, it is a 25 percent increase. In such cases, it is important to give the raw figures. As an adjective, use figures without a hyphen: *a 2 percent rise in the polls*; *a 21 percent drop in value.*

period
A period is used after declarative sentences and:

   a. in decimals and percentages and between dollars and cents: *3.2 million*; *5.09 percent*; *$7.65.*

   b. in most lowercase and capital-lowercase abbreviations: *8 p.m.*; *Jr.*; *Brown v. Board of Education.* But periods are generally not used with abbreviations for metric units or measures: *mm, mph, rpm, Btu.* See also ABBREVIATIONS.

   c. at the end of each item in a series set off by bullets (even if it is not a complete sentence).

   The rules:

   • *Punctuate properly.*
   • *Write simply.*
   • *Type neatly.*

Do not use periods after items in a running summary: *The rules: (1) punctuate properly, (2) write simply and (3) type neatly.*

personnel
This is a collective noun that takes a plural verb: *Their personnel were superior.* Do not use with numerals, as in *three personnel.* See also COLLECTIVE NOUNS.

persons, people
There is no firm rule about which word to use as the plural of *person.* *People* is never wrong. Some writers prefer *persons* for specific numbers. *There were more than 50,000 people at the game. Each of the 50,609 persons who attended received a T-shirt.* When in doubt, let the oral construction be your guide. If it sounds stilted or affected to say, for example, *The crash killed 296 persons,* use *people* instead. Use *people* with indefinite quantifiers: *Most people would say few people were hurt,* not *few persons were hurt.*

phase, faze
A *phase* is a stage or cycle. *They're going through a phase. It goes by the phases of the moon.* To *faze* is to disconcert or embarrass. *The blunder didn't faze her.*

physical appearance
As with all other characteristics, the standard for describing a person's physical appearance or dress is relevance. Obesity, baldness, height, hair color, skin texture, shoe size, skirt length—all may be sensitive, any may cause distress to the person described or to other readers. As with race, age, sexual preference, adoptive status or disability, it may be necessary to discuss details of appearance in a personality profile or in a story where appearance or size is clearly relevant—about athletes, for example, or Miss America contestants or the return of the miniskirt. Apply the relevance test and generally avoid such terms as *fiery redhead, diminutive grandmother, burly truck*

driver etc. See also AGE; RACE AND RACIAL IDENTIFICATION; ADOPTED, ADOPTIVE; HOMOSEXUAL, GAY; DISABLED; SEXISM AND SEX-BASED LANGUAGE.

Pimlico Race Course (Baltimore)

pinch-hit (verb, noun and adjective); *pinch hitter*

pistol
See FIREARMS.

place names
See GEOGRAPHIC NAMES.

plants
See TREES AND PLANTS.

playoff (noun and adjective); *play off* (verb)

plead
The past tense of *plead* is *pleaded*. Do not use *pled*.

plurality
See MAJORITY.

plus
The word is a preposition. It should not be used at the beginning of a sentence as a synonym for *and, moreover* or *furthermore,* which are adverbs, or as a substitute for *also.*

podium, lectern, dais
A *podium* is a low platform upon which one stands or sits, usually for a speech or performance. *The conductor was on the podium.* The slanted table upon which a speaker puts text and microphone is a

lectern. The speaker pounded the lectern as his voice rose. A *dais* is a platform raised above the floor at one end of a hall or room, as for seats of honor. *She was at the dinner but she did not have a seat on the dais.*

pole vaulter*

police

a. Always specify which police force is involved in any story. This is especially important in the Washington area, where there are multiple police forces, some with overlapping jurisdictions.

b. In the District of Columbia, the official name of the force is the Metropolitan Police Department, but D.C. police is acceptable.

c. The police force responsible for protecting foreign diplomats and embassies is the Uniformed Division of the Secret Service, a branch of the U.S. Treasury Department.

d. Capitalize police in the formal name of an organization. Lowercase generic references and plurals. *Fairfax County Police, Maryland State Police, the chief of the U.S. Park Police; D.C. police officers, Maryland and Virginia state police. It took the police 15 minutes to arrive.*

political parties

Party affiliations and geographic bases of members of Congress and other legislative bodies are given in parentheses after the first reference: *Sen. John Warner (R-Va.); Del. Peter Franchot (D-Montgomery); D.C. Council member Hilda Mason (Statehood-At Large).* These designations are omitted in stories that deal entirely with one geographic area or one party: *House Democrats chose Rep. John Smith of Illinois to represent them in the conference.* See also CAPITALIZATION.

politics

Words ending in *-ics*, such as *politics, economics* and *tactics*, may be singular or plural, depending on context: *Politics is my business. Their politics are dirty. Tactics is a science. His tactics are irrational.*

polls

The more important the results of a poll are to a story, the more technical information must be given about the survey data. A casual or general reference, such as *Recent polls in several states show strong support for the farm bill* requires no elaboration. But when the poll itself is the story, details are essential.

Suppose a story said *Nearly 90 percent of American women disapprove of abortion and want the Supreme Court to reverse its decision in Roe v. Wade, a new poll shows.* To assess the validity of such a poll and help the readers understand its significance, the story must give the identity of the poll's sponsor, the dates it was taken, the number of persons interviewed and their characteristics (registered voters, employed, Catholics etc.), the method of polling (telephone, in person etc.) and the margin of sampling error. When findings are likely to be controversial, the story should also give the exact wording of the questions. Consult the director of polling for further guidance.

pornography

Pornography is material written, drawn or photographed primarily to arouse sexual desire in others. On the use of pornographic material in the newspaper, see PROFANE AND VULGAR LANGUAGE.

possessives

See APOSTROPHE.

post office, Postal Service

The organization that delivers the mail is the U.S. Postal Service. Lowercase *post office* as a general term and in references to branch stations. *She went to the post office. He works at the Cleveland Park post office.*

post-

Follow the guidelines given under PREFIXES except for *postgame** and *postseason.**

postpone

See CANCEL.

pre-

Follow the guidelines given under PREFIXES except for *pregame** and *preseason.**

predict

The verb *predict* must be followed by a noun or by a verb in the future tense. *Smith predicts that the nation will face a long period of economic decline. Smith predicted that the nation would face a long period of economic decline. He predicts the Redskins will win. He predicted the Redskins would win.* Do not follow *predict* with a verb in contemporaneous time, as in *Smith predicts that the nation is facing a long period of economic decline.* If it is already happening, his words are not a prediction.

prefixes

    a. In general, hyphenate prefixes except when the hyphen is omitted in Webster's New World Dictionary: *anti-dumping, anti-gun, anti-apartheid, anti-vice,* but *antiaircraft, antibiotic; co-worker* but *costar; pre-convention, pre-surgery,* but *preheat, premeditate.* The objective is clarity. Omission of the hyphen with compounds that are not commonly recognized or standard words produces anomalies such as *antigun, antimale, antibias* and *antiship,* which confuse the

reader—confusion that is aggravated when the words fall at the end of a line and the typesetting computer breaks them after the first syllable.

b. Proper names and official designations take precedence over the dictionary and over Washington Post style. *Anti-Ballistic Missile Treaty.*

c. Use a hyphen if the word that follows the prefix is capitalized: *un-American, anti-Christian.* But note that some proper nouns and their prefixes are run together, in which case there is no hyphen and the proper noun is not capitalized: *transatlantic, antisemitic.* Consult the dictionary for words in this category.

d. Hyphenate when a prefix ends in a vowel and the following word begins with the same vowel, except for *cooperate, coordinate, preempt* and most common verbs beginning with *re-.* The dictionary gives an extensive list of *re-* words that need not be hyphenated, including *reeducate, reelect, reemphasize* and *reenlist.*

e. If a prefix is added to a modifying phrase, the prefix and all the words in the modifier must be hyphenated. Avoid this by recasting the sentence. *Nancy Reagan's anti-drug-abuse campaign; Nancy Reagan's campaign against drug abuse.*

premier
As a noun, use *prime minister* except in headlines and where *premier* is the specific title in English, as in *premier* of an Australian state or a Canadian province. As an adjective, *premier* means foremost.

premiere*
Noun and adjective. Careful writers avoid using it as a verb.

presently
See CURRENTLY.

prestigious

This word has been devalued through overuse. It means having power or influence derived from fame or wealth, having the power to command admiration. Universities and law firms may deserve this description but hotels, suburbs and travel guides generally do not. Try a more precise word: *eminent, powerful, expensive, respected, famous* etc.

prime time

Two words.

Prince William Board of County Supervisors

Not Prince William County Board of Supervisors.

pro-

See PREFIXES.

pro-choice

See RIGHT-TO-LIFE.

profane and vulgar language

a. Words and expressions generally regarded as obscene, profane or blasphemous should be used only with great care. In general, omit them except when they are relevant to the story, as in an article about court rulings on obscenity.

b. In quotations, such words may be published in the rare cases when they are necessary to the understanding of a person or situation, as in an article about a prominent official berating subordinates in harsh language. The classic example was John F. Kennedy's description of business executives as "sons of bitches."

c. Generally, such words should be replaced by *{expletive}* or omitted. Bowdlerized words may be put between brackets. *"They're all {messed} up,"* he said. Do not use initial letters with dashes or ellipses: s--- etc. When in doubt, consult the managing editor or the executive editor. See also QUOTATIONS.

Professional Golfers' Association
Abbreviated PGA. In sports stories, PGA is acceptable on first reference.

professor
The word is abbreviated as a title, but not as an identifier.

> *Prof. Pierre LeGrand of Georgetown University;*
> *Georgetown University French professor Pierre LeGrand;*
> *former American University chemistry professor George Brown.*

When modified by *assistant* or *associate, professor* should be placed after the name: *Pierre LeGrand, assistant professor of French.* See also ABBREVIATIONS and TITLES.

protagonist
The protagonist is the leading character in a drama or story. Strictly speaking, there can be only one, as in "Hamlet," but the word may sometimes be used for more than one, as in "Romeo and Juliet." *Protagonist* is not a synonym for *antagonist.*

proved, proven
The standard past participle of *prove* is *proved*:

> *The prosecutor has proved his case. The theory hasn't been proved.*

Proven may be used as an adjective:

> *She's a proven winner.*

pseudonyms

No pseudonyms or invented names are to be used under any circumstances. If a person cannot be identified, say so and say why but do not make up a name. A nom de guerre such as Abu Nidal may be used if the person in question uses it and is known by it.

punctuation

See separate entries under COMMA, DASH, ELLIPSIS, HYPHEN, QUOTATION MARKS etc. See also NUMERALS.

Pyrrhic victory

A Pyrrhic victory is not just a hollow victory but one in which the victor in a battle suffers such great losses as to be fatally weakened.

Queen Elizabeth II (monarch); *Queen Elizabeth 2* (ship)

question mark

Use a question mark after a direct question but not after an indirect question: *May I go? He asked if he could go.* In multiple questions, generally use a single question mark at the end of the question. *What are your summer plans—to paint, to travel or simply to relax?* But separate question marks may be used after each element for emphasis. *What are your plans? To paint? To travel? Or simply to relax?*

As with the exclamation point, do not use a comma after a question mark unless the question mark is part of a proper noun rather than the ending of a sentence or quote. *"What next?" he asked. His book, "What Next?," was very influential.*

quietly

Quietly is a loaded adverb, often connoting underhanded tactics or questionable motives. In general, the word should be avoided, especially in leads, unless there is clear evidence of duplicitous intent.

quotation marks

1. **Use quotation marks around:**

    a. direct quotations of spoken or written material.

    b. key words and phrases of attributed quotes. Quotation marks are often overused for this purpose; routine phrases should not be quoted. *She called him a "dirty spy."* But *She accused him of being a spy*, not *She accused him of being a "spy."*

    c. titles of essays, articles, plays, operas, dance works, songs, motion pictures, comic strips, works of art, radio and television programs and books other than reference and sacred books. See also SHOWS AND EXHIBITIONS.

    d. titles and fanciful names of musical compositions, but not generic titles identifying the work by type, key signature or instrumentation. See MUSIC.

    e. nicknames inserted in a proper name. *Thomas P. "Tip" O'Neill Jr.; Emil "the Antelope" Verban.* See also NICKNAMES.

    f. misnomers and ironic references. Use quotation marks sparingly for this purpose, as they lack subtlety. It is better to let words convey meaning than to rely on typographical devices. *The "mansion" he told us about turned out to be a three-room cottage. What she called Greenhill Mansion turned out to be a three-room cottage.*

    g. slang, jargon and coined or specialized words not readily understood. Use quotation marks only on first reference. *The train was "deadheaded"—it carried no passengers. Trains are often deadheaded when most of the traffic is moving one way.*

    h. terms that are subjective, or "loaded," or clearly euphemistic or misleading. In these instances, use quotation marks at least on first reference and possibly on subsequent references to make sure the point is clear. *The president's*

*"Star Wars" program; the schools were "separate but equal";
South African "homelands."*

i. words or phrases referred to as such. *The term "gentlemen's
    agreement" is misused. He said "and," not "an." The newspaper
    used "Ms." before her name.*

2. **Do not use quotation marks around:**
   a. names of characters in books, plays, TV programs etc. *He
       was like the Artful Dodger in "Oliver Twist." He played Archie
       in "All in the Family."*

   b. names of reference books: *the World Almanac; Webster's New
       World Dictionary; the Encyclopedia Americana; the Yellow Pages.*

   c. names of sacred books: *the Bible, the Koran, the Torah, the
       Book of Job, the Bhagavad-Gita.*

   d. names of newspapers and periodicals.

   e. interviews and dialogue in question-and-answer format:

       Q: *When did you leave?*
       A: *Late in September.*

   f. names of animals, varieties of plants, ships, teams, games
       or events. *His horse, Dancer II; the Peace rose; a game of
       Monopoly; his boat Our Sal; the Potomac Riverfest.*

   g. the words *yes* and *no* in vote tallies and in other instances
       that signify an affirmative or negative response rather than
       direct quotation. *Among Democrats, 13 voted yes and 11 voted
       no. He begged and begged, but his mother still said no.*

   h. texts of documents, statements etc. printed as separated
       entities.

   i. quotes that have been separated from the rest of the text
       by a typographical device, such as italics or indented mar-
       gins.

3. Sequence and typography

    a. Use double quotation marks in body type, captions, the index and tables of contents, and around quotations within pullout quotes that are indented or otherwise set off from text.

    b. Use single quotation marks in headlines, subheads and logos.

    c. In quotes within quotes, alternate single and double quotes. Separate them with a thin space to avoid breaking them at the end of a line of type.

    d. To form the possessive of a quoted word, include the *'s* within the quotation marks. *I never understood "Twelfth Night's" appeal.*

    e. In extended quotations, use opening marks at the beginning of each paragraph, closing marks only at the conclusion of the material.

    f. Periods and commas go inside quotation marks, colons and semicolons outside.

    g. Exclamation points and question marks go inside or outside quotation marks, depending on whether they apply to the quoted matter or the entire sentence. *"You're out!" the umpire shouted. "Did I hear him ask you, 'Are you married?' " What is the meaning of "snollygoster"?*

    h. No punctuation is used between single and double quotes.

    i. In headlines, names of horses and boats may be shortened and placed within single quotation marks. *'Colors' Takes Oaks; 'Star' on the Rise.*

    j. On the use of brackets and the ellipsis to indicate added or deleted matter, see QUOTATIONS, PARENTHESES AND BRACKETS and ELLIPSIS.

quotations

Quotations should be exact. The words of another person should not be rearranged for more felicitous phrasing. Omissions should be noted by ellipses; insertions should be noted by brackets. Comments or remarks that are issued in printed statements, as by a corporate public relations office, or relayed by third parties, as by a corporate spokesman, should be labeled clearly—not just quoted as if the person had talked to the reporter. Brackets generally should not be used at the beginning or end of quotations. It is preferable simply to open and close the quote where the quoted material begins or ends. Material added by the writer or editor should be outside the quotation marks.

> **POOR:** *"He should never have tried to punt the ball {on the second-period play that led to a fumble}," the coach said.*
>
> **BETTER:** *"He should never have tried to punt the ball" on the second-period play that led to a fumble, the coach said.*

Often it is better to paraphrase a quote, or at least part of it, than to load it down with bracketed explanations.

> "I told them [the Ways and Means Committee] that we [the group] were headed for rough times." (This is accurate but cumbersome.)
>
> He told the Ways and Means Committee that his group was "headed for rough times." (This conveys the same meaning and is much smoother.)

Restructure quoted matter to avoid inaccurate shifts of person or tense. If a person said, *"I've been like this all my life,"* it is inaccurate to write *She said she had "been like this all her life."* Use the full quote:

> *"I've been like this all my life," she told John.*

If a person said, *"I'm determined to achieve my goal this year,"* do not quote her as saying She *"was determined to achieve her goal this year."* Use the full quotation or make it:

> She said she was *"determined to achieve {her} goal this year."*

In direct quotations of spoken material, avoid abbreviations other than *Dr.* Words that are normally abbreviated in writing may actually be stressed for effect by a speaker.

> *"I wanted Colonel Sam Robinson, not Sergeant Sam Robinson,"* he said. *"I'm from Joplin, Missouri, so you'll have to show me,"* she said.

See also PARENTHESES AND BRACKETS.

Quotations of people whose speech is marked by dialect, incorrect grammar or profanity often present difficult choices. Giving the exact words of people who are poorly educated or who are not native speakers of English may be needlessly embarrassing to them. On the other hand, it's foolish, as well as misleading, to alter the words of high school dropouts to make them sound like professors.

In general, try to avoid condescension. Unless difficulties with the language are relevant to the story, as in an article about teaching English to immigrants or a profile of Yogi Berra, it is advisable to correct minor errors of grammar and usage. Such locutions as *hafta, gonna, gotta, whaddsya* and *woulda* should be spelled out in correct form unless they are stressed for effect. The use of *sic* to indicate an error in grammar or spelling is often viewed as condescending, or as belittling the speaker or writer. Avoid it unless it is important to emphasize that the writer or speaker made a mistake.

Irrelevant profanities may be deleted. See also PROFANE AND VULGAR LANGUAGE.

In quotations of written material, the original should be followed exactly in spelling, punctuation and capitalization. Where the style of the original conflicts with Washington Post style, follow the original. If needed, explanatory material may be inserted between brackets.

race and racial identification

   a. In general, race and ethnic background should not be mentioned unless they are clearly relevant. They are obviously relevant in stories about civil rights issues, the problems or achievements of minority groups, cultural history and racial conflict.

   b. Avoid ethnic labels and stereotypes such as *hard-drinking Irishman, tempestuous Latins* or *Chinese fire drill.*

   c. Americans of Mexican, Central American, Spanish-speaking Caribbean or South American background are Hispanic Americans or Hispanics, not Latinos. People from Puerto Rico are Puerto Ricans, but they are Hispanic when grouped with other Hispanics. **Note:** By U.S. government definition, people of Portuguese background, including Brazilians, are not Hispanics. See also PHYSICAL APPEARANCE and ORIENTAL.

racket
The light bat or paddle for all racket sports, including racquetball.

ranging from
This formulation is useful only when an actual range is given. *The guerrillas' weapons ranged from single-shot rifles to heavy artillery. Over the decade, the budget deficit has ranged from $2 million to $6.5 million.* In a sentence such as *They received many wedding presents, ranging from toasters to towels*, there is no range and the expression is not helpful to the reader. Also, avoid such expressions as *in the $200 range.* There is no range. Use *about $200* or *in the $190 to $210 range.*

rank and file (noun); rank-and-file (adjective)

rape

The names of surviving victims of sex crimes are not to be printed without authorization of the executive editor or the managing editor.

re-

See PREFIXES.

Realtor

A *Realtor* is a member of the National Association of Realtors and subscribes to its codes of ethics. The word is a registered trademark. Many real estate brokers and agents are not Realtors. Do not use *realtor* or *Realtor* as a generic word for real estate broker.

recipes

In recipes and other articles about food, units of measurement are spelled out and all quantities are given in numerals: *¼ cup*, *2 cups*, *4 ounces*, *3 teaspoons*. See NUMERALS and FOREIGN WORDS.

redundancies and superfluous words

Many phrases and expressions that appear in the newspaper every day contain redundant, repetitious and unnecessary words. In the following list, the words in italics should generally be omitted:

6 a.m. *in the morning*	*free* gift, *free* pass, *for* free
(or 6 p.m. *in the evening*)	*future* plans
close *personal* friend	*general* consensus (or,
completely eliminated	worse yet,
completely naked or nude	*general* consensus *of*
controversial issue	*opinion*)
definite decision	high *rate of* speed
filled *to capacity*	*in order* to
first began, first *ever*	*invited* guest
for recreation *purposes*	joined *together*

mining *operations*

new record (As in *He set a new record in the race*.)

new recruit

old adage

outer space

past experience, *past* history

protest *against*

qualified expert

razed *to the ground*

reason *why*

remanded *back*

rose *to his feet*

sob *audibly*

strangled *to death*

totally destroyed

true facts

weather *conditions*

were *as follows*

whether *or not*

referendum

A referendum is a vote on a measure or proposition that has been submitted to the electorate for approval. It is not the measure or proposition itself.

> CORRECT: *Fairfax County voters approved the tax increase in a referendum.*

> INCORRECT: *Fairfax County voters approved the tax increase referendum.*

reform

This is a highly subjective word that connotes approval. One legislator's "reform" bill might be anathema to others. Use *revision, overhaul* or other neutral terms.

reformed alcoholic

Do not use this term. Use *recovering alcoholic*.

refute, rebut

To *refute* is to disprove. To *rebut* to is to dispute or counter. Especially in political stories, the word *refute* is best avoided; it implies that the person doing the rebutting has proved his or her case.

religion and the clergy

A person's religious belief or denomination is mentioned only when it is essential to a full understanding of the story.

Avoid casual descriptive references such as *devout Catholic*, *New England Episcopalian*, *Orthodox Jew* etc. Use such terms only when it is clear that they are needed to understand the behavior or incident that is being written about. Make sure they are accurate. For example, not every devout, practicing Jew is an Orthodox Jew. Not all people of Irish descent who have large families are devout Catholics.

Words such as *devout* and *pious* should be used sparingly in any case. A person who performs the external rituals of devotion may in fact be a hypocrite.

The standard reference work on the beliefs, history, organization and membership of religious organizations in the United States is the Yearbook of American and Canadian Churches.

In stories concerning religion or the religious beliefs of individuals, it is often important to distinguish among different groups or organizations within the same framework of belief. For example, the Yearbook of American and Canadian Churches lists 14 organizations of Lutherans in the United States, ranging in membership from 13,000 to nearly 3 million.

The largest denomination in the United States is the Roman Catholic Church. The official names of the other Christian denominations with more than 2 million members:

the African Methodist Episcopal Church

the American Lutheran Church

the Assemblies of God

the Church of God in Christ

the Church of Jesus Christ of Latter-day Saints (the Mormon Church).
  (Note the lowercase *d*.)

the Episcopal Church

the Lutheran Church in America

the Lutheran Church—Missouri Synod

the National Baptist Convention of America

the Presbyterian Church (U.S.A.)

the Southern Baptist Convention

the United Methodist Church

a. In general, identify religious figures and organizations as they identify themselves. Unless indicated otherwise in the Yearbook of American and Canadian Churches or the Official Catholic Directory, members of the Catholic and Episcopal clergy are *priests*. An Episcopal priest in charge of a parish is its *rector*. A Catholic priest in charge of a parish is its *pastor*. Members of the Lutheran clergy are *pastors*. Others in the Christian clergy are generally *ministers*.

b. On first reference, members of the Christian clergy are introduced by the honorific *the Rev.* (for the Reverend) unless they are Christian Scientists, Mormons or Jehovah's Witnesses or unless they hold some higher title, such as *Bishop* or *Cardinal*. Titles other than *the Reverend* are not abbreviated: *Monsignor John Smith*; *Bishop John Smith*; *Cardinal John Smith*. Do not use *Father* as a title for Catholic or Episcopal priests. In the Catholic church, brothers and nuns espouse a religious life but are not members of the clergy and are not *the Rev.*: *Brother John Smith*; *Sister Mary Agnes O'Brien*. On subsequent references to all, use last name only, except for nuns and brothers who use only their religious names: *the Rev. Jerry Falwell*, *Falwell*; *Cardinal Robert McIntyre*, *McIntyre*. *Sister Mary Agnes O'Rourke*, *O'Rourke* (if she uses her family name; otherwise, *Sister Mary Agnes*); *Brother Andrew*.

c. Note that some persons who describe themselves as members of the clergy are not affiliated with any particular church. Unless this question of affiliation is an issue in the story, it is customary to take their word about their clerical status.

d. Members of the clergy who run for political office do not carry the religious title in political stories. *Robert Drinan, a Jesuit priest running for Congress*, not the *Rev. Robert Drinan* or *Father Robert Drinan*; *Jesse L. Jackson*; *Jerry A. Moore Jr.*

e. Jews may be members of Orthodox, Conservative or Reform (not Reformed) congregations. Do not describe one of these types of Judaism as more observant or more devout than others. A member of the Jewish clergy is *Rabbi* on first reference, last name only on subsequent references. See also SYNAGOGUE.

f. In Islam, there is no clergy. No one is ordained in Islam, and no leader of any Moslem organization or congregation should be referred to as *the Rev.* Perhaps the best-known Moslem group in the United States is the World Community of Islam in the West, based in Chicago. Its leader is Wallace D. Muhammad, son of Elijah Muhammad. The group headed by Louis Farrakhan is known as the Nation of Islam, but its teachings and practices differ in important respects from those of mainstream Islam. Do not use the term *Mohammedan*. See also MOSLEM, MUSLIM and AYATOLLAH.

g. A mosque is a building where Moslems gather to pray. Do not say *Moslem mosque*. The Islamic Center of Washington is the official name of the mosque on Massachusetts Avenue NW.

h. Follow dictionary style on capitalization of rites and ceremonies. See CAPITALIZATION, 7f.

repeat

There are a few instances in which *repeat* is acceptable as a noun: *The program was a repeat of one shown earlier.* In general, however, *repeat* should be used only as a verb. The noun is *repetition*.

repertoire, repertory

The words are not interchangeable. A *repertoire* is all the works of drama or music that a performer or company has learned and is prepared to perform, or all the works in a particular category: *the entire repertoire of piano quintets.* A *repertory* is the system of rotating productions of plays, musical works or operas used by repertory companies. A repertory theater company is one in which a permanent company of actors presents plays in rotation.

replete

The word means stuffed, gorged with food. It is not a synonym for or superlative of *complete*.

replica

Not every copy is a replica. Strictly speaking, a replica is made by the original creator of a work, or under his or her supervision. The word may be used if a copy is exact and full size. Otherwise, use *reproduction* or *copy*. *Exact replica* is redundant.

Reserve Officers' Training Corps

ROTC is acceptable on all references. Specify the service: Navy ROTC, Army ROTC, Air Force ROTC.

restaurateur

A person who operates a restaurant is a restaurateur, not a restauranteur.

retired

See FORMER.

Reuter
The news agency is *Reuter* in credit lines and text.

revenue
A collective noun meaning income from all sources, as in Internal Revenue Service. It should not be used in the plural. *The company's revenue from sales and operations rose 12 percent last year.*

revolver
See FIREARMS.

Richter scale
The Richter scale is a gauge of the energy released by an earthquake, as measured by the ground motion recorded on a seismograph. Each increase of one number on the scale, say from 4 to 5, indicates a tenfold increase in magnitude. A quake of magnitude 2 is the smallest normally felt by humans. The highest ever recorded was 8.9. There is no upper limit to the scale.

rif (noun and verb); riffed, riffing
This slang word, an acronym for *reduction in force*, has infiltrated the language, especially in Washington. Use *rif* only when it cannot be avoided, as in quotations. Use *layoff* or *furlough* instead.

rifle
See FIREARMS.

right-handed, right-hander

right-to-life
The terms *right-to-life* and *pro-life* are used by advocates in the abortion controversy to buttress their arguments. They should generally be used as part of an organization's title and in quotations, but not as descriptive adjectives in the text. Use *abortion-rights advocates* for

those who support freedom of choice in the matter, *antiabortion* for those who oppose it.

Ringling Bros. and Barnum & Bailey Circus
That is the name of the show. The formal name of the company, which is based in Washington, is Ringling Brothers—Barnum & Bailey Combined Shows Inc.

Rio Grande
Not Rio Grande River. *Rio* means river.

rob, steal
You rob a person or an institution of property; you steal property.

Robert F. Kennedy Memorial Stadium
Spell out on first reference, except in sports stories. Afterward, RFK Stadium. The stadium is operated by the D.C. Armory Board.

rock-and-roll

Roman numerals
See NUMERALS.

Rosecroft Raceway

Rosh Hashanah*

route
Do not abbreviate, except in headlines, where it is *Rte.*

row house

rushed to a hospital
Avoid this cliché. If the rescue squad dawdles on the way to the hospital, that's news. Use *taken to a hospital*.

Russia, Russian
See SOVIET UNION.

Russian names
Use the endings *-sky* (instead of *-ski*) and *-ov* (instead of *-off*): *Sharansky, Chebrikov*. An exception is made for a prominent or well-known person who used or uses the other form: *Rachmaninoff*. Follow the style of Webster's New World Dictionary: *Sergei Rachmaninoff, Joseph Stalin*. The exception is Alexander Solzhenitsyn.*

In Russian women's names, do not use the Russian feminine ending unless the woman is prominent under her own name: *Viktoria Brezhnev* (not *Brezhneva*); but *ballerina Maya Plisetskaya* (not *Plisetsky*, her husband's name).

Note that Russians commonly refer to each other by given name and patronymic, not last name: *Vladimir Ilyich* (*Lenin*), *Anton Pavlovich* (*Chekhov*), *Mikhail Sergeyeyich* (*Gorbachev*). On first reference, use the initial of the patronymic: *Mikhail S. Gorbachev*. On second reference in English text, use the last name, not the patronymic: *Gorbachev*. See also FOREIGN NAMES.

7-Eleven store

saccharin, saccharine
Saccharin (noun) is a sugar substitute. *Saccharine* (adjective) means containing or producing sugar, or syrupy sweet.

saint
Abbreviate in place names and names of churches and institutions but not in the names of canonized persons: *St. Paul, Minn.*; *St. Paul's Church*; *the epistles of Saint Paul*. Exception: *Saint John, New Brunswick*.

sanction
The verb can mean approve or disapprove, so it is best avoided.

saving, savings

This noun has singular and plural forms. Do not use *a savings* as in *The reductions meant a savings of $1 million*. As an adjective, the plural form is commonly used in financial stories: *savings institutions, the savings and loan industry*.

scheme

Writers of British or Australian background use the word to mean plan or program: *The government's scheme to build roads through the mountains*. In American English, the word often implies illegal actions or conspiracies and is best avoided except when that implication is deliberate.

school board

The term is capitalized only when it is part of an official name, as in Virginia jurisdictions: *The Fairfax County School Board*. In Maryland jurisdictions and the District of Columbia, the school board is the Board of Education. *The Prince George's County Board of Education*.

scissors

This is a plural noun. Do not use *scissor* or *a scissors*. The common household item is a pair of scissors.

scorecard*

scores

See NUMERALS.

Scot, Scots, Scottish, Scotch

A *Scot* or *Scotsman* is a native of Scotland. The *Scots* are the people of Scotland. The adjective is *Scottish*. The adjective *Scotch* should be used only in relation to certain well-known items: whisky (without the *e*), broth, terriers. The verb *scotch* means stamp out, put an end to.

Sears, Roebuck and Co.
See DEPARTMENT STORES.

self-confessed
The expression is redundant. Only the person involved can confess. Omit *self-*.

semi-
See PREFIXES.

semicolon
The semicolon separates two or more independent clauses while keeping them in the same sentence. *The Smiths had six children; the Joneses had eight.* Use semicolons sparingly. Periods or colons are usually better in news stories. But semicolons are required:

a. to separate items in a series that already contains commas or might otherwise be confusing. When semicolons are used instead of commas in a series, they are used between all sets of elements, including the last two: *He demonstrated the Model A, his favorite; the Model B; and the Model C.*

b. to separate two sentences in headlines: *13 Killed in Train Wreck; Loose Rail Blamed*

Note that although joining two independent clauses with a comma usually forms what is called a run-on sentence, it is acceptable to join short, direct independent clauses with commas rather than semicolons: *I came, I saw, I conquered. Sometimes you win, sometimes you lose.*

sensuous, sensual

Sensuous means experienced through any of the senses. *Sensual* means carnal or worldly.

sergeant major

The plural is *sergeants major*.

series

The word is often unnecessary when used as part of the expression *a series of*. In sentences such as *They held a series of meetings to discuss the problem* and *She proposed a series of measures for dealing with the issue*, the words *a series of* should be omitted.

sewage, sewers

Sewage is waste matter. The pipes and pumps constructed to handle sewage are sewerage. *The county installed a sewerage system* (or *sewage treatment system*) *to get rid of the sewage*. Sewer system refers to underground pipes only, not the complete network of pipes and treatment plants.

sexism and sex-based language

This is an area in which our language has changed dramatically over the past 20 years as we have tried to eliminate invidious sex-based terms and phrases that no longer reflect our society. Often this transformation has been effortless, as in the substitution of *ordinary person* for *ordinary man*. But sometimes it has presented a new set of difficulties that we have not yet resolved.

If, for example, *his* is no longer acceptable as a generic possessive pronoun, as in *Everyone has his umbrella*, what should replace it? *Everyone has their umbrella* is grammatically incorrect. *Everyone has his or her umbrella* sounds stilted. This particular example has an easy solution: *Everyone has an umbrella*. But not all questions are so readily answered. *Everyone has his own way of doing things. Her own way? Their own way?*

The difficulty is compounded by the fact that many people accept or even demand specifically feminine forms of some nouns (*chairwoman, countess,*) but reject them in other nouns (*stewardess, comedienne*). There are no rules that will or can be applied in every situation, but the following guidelines may help avoid needless sex-based distinctions.

The basic idea is to treat all persons the same in all areas of coverage and to avoid condescension and stereotypes.

a. Use generic terms for occupations or groups of people unless it would be awkward or artificial:

Traditional	*Preferable Alternative*
alumnus, alumna	graduate
businessman	business executive, business manager
college boys, coeds	students
congressman	member of Congress, representative
councilman	council member
fireman	firefighter
garbage man	garbage collector
mailman	letter carrier
man in the street	person in the street
newsman	reporter, journalist
policeman	police officer
stewardess	flight attendant
workman	worker

b. For titles, when referring to specific individuals, use the titles they give themselves: *Chairman Mary Jones* or *Chairwoman Mary Jones*, whichever she uses; *shop steward Joan Smith.* When referring to such positions generally, avoid coined terms such as *chairone*; use the commonly accepted form. *The group caucused briefly to elect a spokesman. Joan Smith, spokeswoman for the group. The company will respond to the charges on Thursday, according to a spokesman (not spokesperson).* See also CHAIRMAN and SPOKESMAN.

c. Some words ending in -*man* are unavoidable. They have no gender-free alternative and are used for women as well as men: *midshipman, freshman, baseman* as in first baseman, *lineman* as in telephone lineman, *foreman* (of a jury); *ombudsman.* Similarly, some words—especially words describing women—are gender-specific but cannot be avoided because there is no credible alternative: *mistress, seamstress.* Do not coin words such as *foreperson* or *ombudsperson* in an attempt to avoid these terms.

d. Do not use gender-based qualifiers with occupations unless pertinent: *lawyer*, not *woman lawyer*; *nurse*, not *male nurse*; *model*, not *male model*. Especially in writing about women, avoid references to family status unless relevant. A sentence such as *Ruth Johnson, who was a grandmother at 33, knows all about teenage pregnancy* is obviously acceptable. But a sentence such as *The only passenger injured was Joan Smith, a 50-year-old grandmother*, may be offensive.

e. Expressions that perpetuate sex-based stereotypes, especially of women, should be avoided: *prim as a schoolmarm, stern as a librarian*. References to personal appearance—blond, diminutive, blue-eyed—should generally be omitted unless clearly relevant to the story.

   See also PHYSICAL APPEARANCE.

f. On second reference, women as well as men are generally referred to by last name only. Exceptions are made for obituaries, for the spouses of the president of the United States and other heads of state and prominent individuals when they are mentioned only in their spousal role (the wife of West German Chancellor Helmut Kohl is *Mrs.*

Kohl, not *Frau Kohl*), and for individuals known by their titles, such as Queen Elizabeth II, Pope John Paul and the Dalai Lama. See also TITLES; GENDER and MR., MRS., MISS, MS.

shambles

Literally, a *shambles* is a slaughterhouse. Figuratively, any scene of great disorder or violence may be *a shambles* but not *in a shambles*.

ships and boats

See BOAT, SHIP.

short-handed

The hyphen is omitted in hockey stories: *a shorthanded goal*.

shotgun, shot

See FIREARMS.

shows and exhibitions

a. Capitalize and use quotation marks around names of shows, exhibitions and events that are unique or very specific: *"American Art Deco: The Early Years"*; *"Designing Interiors on a Limited Budget"*; *"Five Centuries of Islamic Art."*

b. Omit the quotation marks around annual shows or sales or events that are generic in nature: *The Paris Auto Show, the 17th annual Hunt Valley Antiques Show, the K Street Home Improvement Show. The Picasso show at the museum*; *"Picasso: The Sculptures."*

shutout (noun); shut out (verb)

sic

Use this sparingly and with caution. See QUOTATIONS.

single out

Single means one. To single out means to select or cite one of a group. Avoid such constructions as *He singled out Britain, France and Italy for special praise.*

Sir, Dame

These honorifics are bestowed upon baronets and persons who have been knighted by the British monarch: *Sir Harold Wilson, Dame Margot Fonteyn.* On second reference, use the last name only: *Wilson, Fonteyn* (not *Sir Harold* etc.). See also TITLES.

sitcom

This colloquial contraction of situation comedy has worked its way into the language but is still listed by the dictionary as a colloquialism. It is acceptable in reviews or feature stories where show business slang or television industry jargon is clearly appropriate. In other text, use *TV comedy* or *situation comedy. At that network, where the level of taste has never been lower, they think of "Taxi" as a sitcom with a heart. The government's effort to balance the budget without raising taxes is beginning to resemble a TV comedy.*

-size

In compound adjectives, use *-size,* not *-sized. Olympic-size pool, king-size bed.* Lowercase size designations: *Her dress was a size 8.*

Smokey Bear

Not Smokey the Bear.

snafu

This is a slang term at best, originally an acronym for an expression containing an obscenity. Its use should be restricted to quotations. If it must appear in text, use it only as a noun, never as a verb.

snuck

A colloquialism at best. It should be used only in direct quotation. The past tense of *sneak* is *sneaked*.

somewhat

This adverb means to some extent or degree, a little: *She's somewhat late, as usual.* Its use as a noun followed by *of* should be avoided: *He's somewhat of a joker.* Make it *something of a joker.*

Soviet Union

a. The Union of Soviet Socialist Republics, or Soviet Union, consists of 15 constituent republics, of which Russia is the largest in population. *Russian* refers to the language and people of one of many ethnic groups in the Soviet Union. *Russia* and *Russians* should not be used as synonyms for Soviet Union and Soviet citizens or Soviet people. Natives of the other Soviet Republics—Uzbekistan, Armenia, Georgia, Estonia etc.—are not Russians.

b. *Soviet* as a noun is a group, not an individual: *the Supreme Soviet, local soviets in Siberia.* In headlines, however, *Soviet* may be used to refer to an individual because it is preferable to *Russian*: Foreign Minister Eduard Shevardnadze is a Soviet, for headline purposes, but he is not a Russian.

space shuttle

Lowercase the aircraft, capitalize the name. *The space shuttle Discovery; the space shuttle landed safely.*

Spanish and Hispanic names

Many people of Hispanic background who live in the United States and Canada have Anglicized the spellings of their names, omitting accent marks, hyphens, matronymics etc. Spell the names of such people as they spell them. Otherwise, follow these guidelines:

a. Hispanic men use two-part family names. They use the father's last name and then the mother's, sometimes linked by *y*. In second reference, only the father's name is used: *Raul Jimenez Lopez, Jimenez*; *the Spanish philosopher Jose Ortega y Gassett, Ortega*. Some Hispanic men use both names or hyphenate the names. In such cases, both parts are used on second reference: *Marcos Perez Jimenez, Perez Jimenez*; *Hector Garcia-Godoy, Garcia-Godoy*. Residents of this country and prominent individuals abroad may be known by a single last name: *Spanish Prime Minister Felipe Gonzalez*. But U.N. Secretary General Javier Perez de Cuellar on second reference is Perez de Cuellar.

b. When a Hispanic woman marries, she retains her family name and adds her husband's. Maria Perez, upon marrying Luis Gonzalez, becomes Maria Perez de Gonzalez. In this country she may call herself Maria Gonzalez. The Hispanic forms of the surname should be used if the individual's preference is not known. See also ACCENT MARKS.

species

Capitalize the generic, lowercase the specific name, and italicize both words. *Homo sapiens.* See also TREES AND PLANTS

spelling

a. For English words not listed in this stylebook, use the spelling given in Webster's New World Dictionary, Third College Edition (1988).

b. Where that dictionary gives more than one spelling, use the one for which a full definition is given: *doughnut*, not *donut*; *straitjacket*, not *straightjacket*. Where alternative spellings are given equally, use the one listed first: *impostor*, not *imposter*; *glamour*, not *glamor*.

c. Where the dictionary uses diphthongs, use them: *archae-ology, subpoena*. Where they are omitted, omit them: *or-thopedics*.

d. Exceptions to dictionary spelling are noted in this style-book with an asterisk (*). Accent marks are generally omit-ted for English words: see ACCENT MARKS. See also PREFIXES; COMPOUND WORDS; GEOGRAPHIC NAMES; FOREIGN WORDS. The words marked with an asterisk in this stylebook:

adrenaline	halftime
adviser	home town (noun) (see
ambiance	this entry)
angst	market basket
any more	matzoh
babysitter	molotov cocktail
ballclub	pole vaulter
Beaux-Arts	postgame
breaststroke	postseason
catalogue	pregame
chateaus	premiere
citizens band	preseason
Court of St. James's	Rosh Hashanah
couturier (not italicized)	scorecard
crosscheck (in hockey	Solzhenitsyn, Alexander
stories only)	switch hitter
decor	taekwondo
detente	Third World
en route	time out (see this entry)
facade	vice president
Federal (the architectural)	weightlifter, weightlifting
period only)	working woman
First Lady	Zip code
french fries	

spiral

A spiral curve is two-dimensional, as in one drawn on paper. In three-dimensional form, such a curve is a helix. However, *spiral* is commonly used for three-dimensional objects, as in spiral staircase. Note that a spiral may go up or down. When inflation or development or the birth rate are described as spiraling, it is necessary to say in which direction.

split infinitive

No grammatical rule prohibits splitting the infinitive. According to the Oxford Guide to the English Language, adherence to such an "artificial rule" leads to "unnecessarily contorted sentences. Rather, it is recommended that a split infinitive should be avoided by placing the adverb before or after the infinitive, unless this leads to clumsiness or ambiguity. If it does, one should either allow the split infinitive to stand, or recast the sentence." The Oxford Guide gives examples from well-known authors:

> *What could it be like to actually live in France?* (Kingsley Amis)
>
> *It would be an act of gratuitous folly to, as he had put it to Mildred, make trouble for himself at this stage.* (Iris Murdoch)

Both are acceptable. The objective is to achieve clarity and rhythm and to avoid ambiguity.

spokesman, spokeswoman

Use *spokesman* as the generic term and in references to specific male persons. Use *spokeswoman* in references to specific females, unless they specify otherwise. *Margaret Tutwiler is the State Department spokesman.* Do not use *spokesperson* except in quotations. *This organization needs an official spokesman. Ann Brown, a spokeswoman for the group, denied the charges.* See also SEXISM AND SEX-BASED LANGUAGE.

sports words and terms
Many commonly used sports words and expressions are included in these listings. Consult the Sports desk for words not listed here or in Webster's New World Dictionary. For style on sports scores, see NUMERALS.

St. Albans School for Boys; St. Alban's Episcopal Church

St. Elizabeths Hospital

St. John's Episcopal Church, Lafayette Square
This is the official name of the "church of the presidents."

stanch, staunch
Stanch is a verb meaning stop the flow of, cut off.

Staunch is an adjective meaning steadfast. He said it was time to stanch the flood of usage errors. Even the government's Operation Staunch was misnamed, he said.

steelworkers
One word. See UNIONS.

stock prices
Express them numerically. Values of less than $1 are given in fractions, not decimals. The stock closed yesterday at $11.87½. In stories about stock market activity, prices are given without the dollar. General Motors fell 2½ points, to 37¼.

straitjacket

strikeout (noun); strike out (verb)

strip search (noun); strip-search (verb)

sub-
See PREFIXES.

subpoena

Sudan
Not *the Sudan*. Omit the article.

suffixes
a. Some suffixes take hyphens, some do not. In general, follow Webster's New World Dictionary.

b. Always hyphenate to avoid tripling a letter, as in *bell-like*. Do not hyphenate words with *able* or suffixes that are not words in themselves, even with coined words or proper names: *hillbillyness*, *doable*, *Kafkaesque*.

c. If the dictionary gives no guidance, the following suffixes are run in with root words of one or two syllables: *like*, *wide*, *goer*, *going*, *maker*, *making*, *proof*. They are hyphenated or separated when the root word is of three or more syllables: *worldwide*, *university-wide*; *lawmaker*, *decision maker*. See also HYPHEN and COMPOUND WORDS.

sustain
To sustain is to support, maintain or prolong. Injuries are suffered or incurred, not sustained.

switch hitter*

synagogue
A synagogue is a house of worship for Jews. *Jewish synagogue* is redundant. The word is not part of the proper name: *Adas Israel synagogue*.

T-shirt

table
As a verb, this is used in the United States to mean postpone. In Britain, it has the opposite meaning—to put on the table for consideration, to bring up.

tactics
Like other words ending in *-ics,* tactics may be singular or plural. See POLITICS.

*taekwondo**

taps
Lowercase. No quotation marks. It takes a plural verb. *At the ceremony, taps were sounded.*

taste and sensitivity
In demanding that the contents of The Washington Post be "fit reading for the young as well as for the old," Eugene Meyer was addressing the subject of taste and of readers' sensitivities. Standards of taste and morality are subject to cultural change, but certain principles in the use of the language endure.

Defamatory or prejudicial words and phrases that perpetuate racial, religious or ethnic stereotypes are impermissible. Language that gives needless offense to certain groups is to be avoided. For guidance on specific matters, see AGE; DISABLED; HOMOSEXUAL; PHYSICAL APPEARANCE; PROFANE AND VULGAR LANGUAGE; RACE AND RACIAL IDENTIFICATION; RELIGION AND THE CLERGY; and SEXISM AND SEX-BASED LANGUAGE.

teenage, teenager
Do not use *teen* as a synonym for teenager, except in headlines.

telephone company

There is no longer a single "telephone company." Specify: *the Chesapeake & Potomac Telephone Co., Nynex, Bell South, MCI Communications* etc.

telephone numbers

Area codes are in parentheses: (202) 334-6000. Use hyphens for 800 numbers: Dial 1-800-BIG DEAL.

temperature

Use figures for all temperatures except zero. When the temperature is below zero, use the word *below,* not a minus sign:

It was 12 degrees below zero by dawn.

If for some reason a temperature scale other than Fahrenheit is used, specify, and give the Fahrenheit equivalent.

The temperature at the airport was 36 degrees Celsius (97 Fahrenheit).

Avoid the expression *subfreezing temperatures.* All temperatures below 32 degrees Fahrenheit are freezing.

that, which

The pronoun *that* introduces a restrictive or defining clause that cannot be omitted from the sentence without losing the meaning. *Which* introduces a nonessential or parenthetical clause, set off by commas, which could be omitted.

The proposal that he made last week is already outdated. (All we know about this proposal is that he made it last week. To omit the clause would omit the only definition of the proposal we have.)

The proposal, which he made last week, is already outdated. (We have already learned something about the proposal in a previous reference. The clause between commas tells us something new but is not essential to understand which proposal is being talked about.)

When in doubt, it is often useful to read a sentence aloud. If you hear yourself pausing before the relative pronoun, it probably should be *which* and the clause should be set off by commas. See also COMMA.

theater, theatre
The generic term is *theater*. Use *theatre* only in proper names of specific theaters that use it: *Ford's Theatre, the theater where Lincoln was shot.*

thousand, a thousand
See MILLION.

till, until
The words are interchangeable. Do not use *'til*.

time
    a. In timed events, spell out the words *hours, minutes and seconds* on first reference:

      The winning time was 3 minutes 26.1 seconds.
      She ran the marathon in 2 hours 31 minutes 25.8 seconds.
      The Redskins had to punt with 1 minute 7 seconds remaining.

    Use numerals only thereafter.

      The previous record was 3:26.4. Only 1.07 remained when they punted.

    See also NUMERALS.

    b. When giving a time or making a comparison with another time zone, use *Eastern time, Pacific time* etc. These designations are abbreviated when contained within parentheses. *The plane left Los Angeles at 11 p.m. Pacific time (2 a.m. Friday EDT).* See also DATELINES.

time element

In general, the time element in daily stories is placed directly after the main verb or verb phrase: *The Montgomery County Council voted yesterday . . . President Bush will travel to Geneva Monday . . . An Alexandria jury convicted three women yesterday of fraud and conspiracy charges growing out of the city's procurement scandal.*

But this formation may be changed when necessary for clarity. In a sentence such as *Virginia State Police arrested three men, including two Marines from Quantico, and charged them with the robbery of an Arlington bank* the time element may precede the verb. *Virginia State Police last night arrested three men* etc.

In feature stories and for stylistic effect, the time element may be placed anywhere in the sentence consistent with clarity. *Last year candidate George Bush said, "Read my lips." Yesterday President George Bush said, "Read this budget."*

The week begins on Sunday and ends on Saturday. A story in the Sunday paper referring to *this week* means the week beginning that day.

Be careful with expressions such as *last April* or *next fall*. If a story published in September says *The school opened last April* does that mean five months ago or 17 months ago? For clarity, specify: *The school opened in April* (if it is in the same year as publication) or *The school opened in April 1988* (if it was the preceding year).

See also DATELINES.

time out, timeouts, timeout*

When used with verbs of expression, *time out* is two words. *He called time out. "Time out," she said.* Otherwise, one word: *The Redskins used a timeout; they have two timeouts remaining.*

titles

a. Official, hierarchical and political titles are capitalized when they precede a name. Job descriptions that are not formal titles are lowercase. *President John Black, Senate Majority Leader Mary White, Prince George's County Executive William Brown, D.C. Mayor Marion Barry, Redskins Coach Joe Gibbs, Montgomery County Council secretary Joan Green, Pan Am baggage handler Joe Andrews; Executive Director Mary Johnson, project director Mary Johnson.*

b. In general, titles precede the name, job descriptions follow it: *Ferris & Co. Chairman John Smith; Mary Brown, a Ferris & Co. analyst; Secretary of the Army William Johnson; John Williams, an Army explosives expert; Teamsters President Jimmy Hoffa; Sam Jones, a Teamsters official.*

c. Some descriptions that are not formal titles are recognized as if they were titles and may precede the name but are not capitalized. Spokesman is the most common example: *White House spokesman Marlin Fitzwater.* But if a group has more than one spokesman it is preferable to set the word off between commas: *A State Department spokesman, Robert Brown; James Williams, a spokesman for IBM.*

d. Lowercase titles that denote only membership: *commission member John Black, CBS board member Mary White, City Council member Robert Green, Georgia delegate (to a convention) William White.*

e. In general, references to individuals, job descriptions and other descriptions should follow the name, not precede it as if they were titles. *At the shopping center, the candidate shook the hands of John Smith, a choreographer; Mary Brown, a bookkeeper, and Fred Johnson, a meatpacker.* (Not *choreographer John Smith, bookkeeper Mary Brown* etc.) *Interviewed outside the polling place, John Williams, a college instructor, and Mary White, an architect, said they voted for the Democrat.*

(Not *college instructor John Williams* etc.) In accounts of a single event or performance where many members of one enterprise are named, their roles may be used as if they were titles, lowercase and preceding the name. *Credit for the show's success goes to choreographer John Smith and conductor May Brown. Pilot Bill Smith and flight attendant Jenny Williams said the plane lost power in two engines.*

f.   Titles, like other words, should not be expected to perform two grammatical functions in a sentence at the same time. In a sentence such as *The report was released by Air Force spokesman Capt. Bill Smith* or *The group that seized power was led by Defense Minister Lt. Gen. Juan Sanchez*, the job descriptions—spokesman, defense minister—are both noun and modifier, which is why the sentences are uncomfortable to read aloud. Broadcast style calls for placing all titles, descriptions and modifiers before a name, but in a newspaper such modifiers should be set off by commas. *The report was released by an Air Force spokesman, Capt. Bill Smith. The group that seized power was led by Lt. Gen. Juan Sanchez, the defense minister.* For simplicity's sake, titles denoting elected political office may be placed before the name and abbreviated even when modified: *Georgia's Democratic Gov. Bruce Jones*; *Utah Sen. Ann Brown*.

g.   Capitalize sobriquets: *Sultan of Swat Babe Ruth*; *First Lady Barbara Bush, the First Lady*; *Benny Goodman, the King of Swing*. Note: Do not use *Drug Czar* in reference to the national drug policy director.

h.   Lowercase titles standing alone: *The secretary of defense, the pope, the prince, the chairman.* Titles of nobility are capitalized in references to a specific individual, lowercase standing alone. *The Queen of England, the queen* (there is only one Queen of England, but there are other queens); *the Duke of York, the duke; the Earl of Snowdon, the earl.*

i.   Lowercase and spell out nonmilitary titles used with *ex-, former, retired* and *the late: ex-senator Mary White, former professor John Green, the late governor Andrew Williams of Virginia.* An exception is made for military ranks because officers who retire technically retain their rank: *retired Air Force Maj. Gen. Andrew Brown.* Do not use the form *Maj. Gen. Andrew Brown (USAF ret.)*

j.   Lowercase derivatives: *presidential, senatorial, mayoral, papal, naval.*

k.   Long or unwieldy titles should be placed after the name and lowercase: *John White, deputy assistant secretary of state for East Asian affairs.*

l.   Especially in Britain, some persons are known only by their titles. The titles become their names. Anthony Armstrong-Jones became Lord Snowdon when Queen Elizabeth II made him the Earl of Snowdon. Such persons retain the title on subsequent reference: *Lord Snowdon, Prince Charles.* But persons who have the honorific titles *Sir* and *Dame* are referred to by last name only on second reference: *Sir Harold Wilson, Wilson; Dame Margot Fonteyn, Fonteyn.*

m. See also PROFESSOR; GOVERNOR; RELIGION AND THE CLERGY; ABBREVIATIONS.

Tomb of the Unknowns (not Unknown Soldier)

tomorrow
Do not use in datelined stories. It confuses the reader. Specify the day of the week.

town house

trade names and brands

Successful trade names and brand names often are absorbed into the language as generic terms for the products they represent. But the manufacturers of these products own the names and are legally protected against their use as generic names for the products of others.

a. In general, do not use a trade name for a generic product unless you know that the product bears that name and there is some reason to mention the brand. Not all facial tissues are Kleenex, not all scouring pads are Brillo, not all jeans are Levi's.

b. Some words that began as trade names have made their way into the language and may be used generically: *escalator, linoleum, nylon, trampoline, yo-yo, zipper*. These are lowercase in Webster's New World Dictionary.

c. Some trade names and brands are so successful that there is no generic synonym: *Frisbee, Gatorade, Kool-Aid, Laundromat, Velcro, Wiffle ball*. These should be capitalized, as they are in the dictionary. Aside from these, the best practice is to use the generic term unless there is some reason to mention the trade name.

Common Trade Names	*Generic Synonyms*
Alka-Seltzer	antacid tablet
Baggies	plastic bags
Band-Aid	plastic bandage
ChapStick	lip balm, lip ointment
Clorox	bleach
Cyclone fence	chain-link fence
Cuisinart	food processor
Day-Glo	fluorescent material
Fiberglas	fiber glass

Formica	laminated plastic
Kitty Litter	cat litter
Naugahyde	vinyl-coated fabric
Ping-Pong	table tennis
Plexiglas	clear plastic
Q-Tip	cotton swab
Realtor	real estate agent
Saran wrap	plastic wrap
Scotch tape	cellophane tape
Seeing Eye dog	guide dog
Sheetrock	drywall, wallboard
Technicolor	color
Vaseline	petroleum jelly
Xerox	photocopier

d. Two trade names that present special difficulties are *Jeep* and *Styrofoam*. They are commonly used as generic terms but are in fact trade names. Other manufacturers make similar products that are not Jeeps or Styrofoam. Use *jeep* for military vehicles. Otherwise, use the brand name only for the specific brand, Jeep. Use *off-road vehicle, four-wheel drive vehicle* or the rival brand name (Land Rover etc.), in place of *Jeep*. According to the manufacturer, Styrofoam is never used in plastic cups, so there is no such thing as a Styrofoam cup. But everyone calls them Styrofoam cups, and eventually that will be the generic term. Capitalize *Styrofoam*. In generic references, use plastic foam.

e. In any trade or brand name, only the first letter is capitalized.

f. For more information, consult the United States Trademark Association in New York or the American Intellectual Property Law Association in Arlington, Va.

trans-
See PREFIXES.

trees and plants
For spelling and capitalization of common trees and plants, follow the style of Webster's New World Dictionary: *Scotch pine, Dutch elm, bluegrass*. Where a tree or plant is not listed, lowercase the names of plants but capitalize proper nouns or adjectives that occur in the name: *white Dutch clover*. If a botanical name is used, capitalize the first word only: *blue azalea (Callicarpa americana)*.

trooper, trouper
A *trooper* is a state police officer or member of the cavalry. A *trouper* is a member of a theatrical troupe. *She was sick but she went on anyway, like a real trouper.*

Truman, Harry S.
Use the period even though the *S* doesn't stand for anything. Truman used it.

try
It takes *to*, not *and*, to introduce the following verb. *We're going to try to win for the home fans* not *try and win*.

Tysons Corner
Also Tysons Corner Center (not Shopping Center or Mall); Tysons II Galleria.

Ugly American
The term is widely misused. In the 1958 novel by William J. Lederer and Eugene Burdick, the person known as the Ugly American was the hero, the one who understood the local culture and helped the people. He was not the arrogant, culturally tone-deaf American or boorish tourist whom the expression is often used to describe.

ultra-

As a political or religious label, this prefix should be used only when there is indisputable evidence to support it. It connotes excessive or extreme positions. Terms such as *ultra-conservative* convey value judgments that a newspaper may not wish to make. See also PREFIXES.

un-

See PREFIXES.

under-

See COMPOUND WORDS. *Undersecretary* is one word.

undocumented

When used to describe immigrants, this is a euphemism that obscures an important fact—that they are in this country illegally. In general, use *illegal immigrant* (but not *illegal alien*. The word *alien* is repugnant to some people). Terms such as *undocumented worker* may be used for the sake of variety.

UNESCO

The acronym is acceptable on first reference to the United Nations Educational, Scientific and Cultural Organization. The full name should be given at some point in a story.

UNICEF

Acceptable on all references to the United Nations Children's Fund.

unions

Names of labor unions should always be checked. The formal names of labor organizations may be condensed to conventional short forms. Do not capitalize the word *union* if it is not part of the organization's name. The word *workers* in the name of a union does not take an apostrophe: *the Amalgamated Clothing and Textile Workers Union of*

America; the Textile Workers union; the International Brotherhood of Teamsters, Chauffeurs, Warehousemen and Helpers of America; the International Brotherhood of Teamsters; the Teamsters union. Steelworkers is one word. Other combinations with *workers* are two words: *the United Mine Workers, auto workers, the United Auto Workers.*

unique
It means one of a kind, the one and only. Nothing can be *more unique, less unique* or *very unique.*

United Press International
Spell out in credit lines, not UPI. In text, United Press International on first reference, then UPI.

United States
    a. The name of this country is the United States (not America). It is spelled out when used as a noun, except in headlines. It is generally abbreviated when used as an adjective: *U.S. Army, U.S. policy, the U.S. Court of Appeals, U.S. Postal Service.* Do not use periods when the abbreviation is included as part of the name of a government agency: *USIA, USS Stark.* Use USA in direct quotations only. See also ABBREVIATIONS, 2a.

    b. Citizens of this country may be referred to as Americans, except when they are being specifically distinguished from aliens or from nationals of other countries: *The victims were all Americans. One of the survivors said he was a U.S. citizen.*

unless and until
The expression is redundant. Omit *and until.*

up to . . . or more
This construction, increasingly common in advertisements and bureaucratic reports, is to be avoided because it is meaningless. *The commission said the city could save up to $1 million or more* conveys no information about how great the saving could be. It could be $1 million, or more, or less.

verbal, oral
Verbal means related to words, anything written or spoken. *Oral* means spoken, as opposed to written. Any communication in words—as opposed to visual forms such as signal flags or cave paintings—is verbal. But a spoken communication as opposed to a written one is oral. *The president decided his message had to be delivered orally, so he invited the committee chairmen to lunch.*

veterans
Millions of men and women have served in the armed forces and are proud to be veterans. Be alert to their feelings when describing a criminal or other unsavory character as an *ex-Marine, former Green Beret* etc. Unless it is directly relevant, as when combat training or knowledge of military weaponry is involved in a crime, the military association should be omitted.

versus
Spell out in quotations of spoken material. *"It's going to be the Lions versus the Bears for the championship,"* she said. Otherwise, abbreviate as *vs.*, except *v.* in legal citations. *It's Safeway vs. Giant in a new price war. He cited Baker v. Carr in support of his argument.*

*vice president**

Vietnam Veterans Memorial

Vietnam War

Vietnamese names

a. With very few exceptions, Vietnamese individuals on second reference use the last name, which is the given name. Ngo Dinh Diem was of the Ngo family but he was President Diem. Tran Van Don is of the Tran family but is Don, his given name, on second reference. Gen. Vo Nguyen Giap was Giap. The best-known exception was Ho Chi Minh, who was Ho on second reference.

b. In Vietnam, a married woman generally uses her own name, not her husband's, but there have been prominent exceptions. The wife of Ngo Dinh Nhu was known as Madame Nhu. The leftist politician Mrs. Ngo Ba Thanh was the wife of Ngo Ba Thanh. In this country, many Vietnamese women follow American custom and use the husband's name. Tuan Duc Dang and his wife are Mr. and Mrs. Tuan Duc Dang and both are Dang on second reference unless the wife prefers to be known by her own name.

c. Some well-known Vietnamese place names are one word: Vietnam, Hanoi, Haiphong, Pleiku. Most are two or three words: Can Tho, Ban Me Thuot. Use the spellings in the National Geographic Atlas of the World except for Pleiku, Kontum and Ban Me Thuot.

Virginia Polytechnic Institute and State University

The formal name of the state university in Blacksburg. Virginia Tech may be used in all references except when the full name is emphasized for effect.

vote totals

See NUMERALS.

Walter Reed Army Medical Center

warm-up (noun, adjective); **warm up** (verb)

Washington Cathedral

The Gothic edifice on Mount St. Alban in Northwest Washington is the Cathedral of Sts. Peter and Paul or, informally, the Washington Cathedral. It is not the National Cathedral or Washington National Cathedral. Note, however, that the school for girls affiliated with the cathedral is the National Cathedral School.

Washington Convention Center

The Convention Center, the center. Not D.C. Convention Center.

Washington Dulles International Airport

This is the official name of the airport in Northern Virginia. *Dulles International Airport* is acceptable on all references except when the official name is to be emphasized. As geographic modifier, use Dulles Airport: *the Dulles Airport development corridor.*

Washington Metropolitan Area Transit Authority

Official name of the regional authority that operates the bus and rapid rail systems. In most references, *Metro* is preferred. *The Metro board, Metro officials; Metrorail; the Metrobus system. The flood halted all Metro bus and rail service.* Standing alone, *the Metro* means the train.

Washington, Washington area

These terms may be used in general references to the metropolitan area: *People in Washington are more relaxed than people in New York. Washington area consumers have money to spend.* In references to the city and its government as opposed to the entire area, use District or D.C.: *District roads were clogged by snow. D.C. officials denied that the roads were clogged by snow. After visiting Mount Vernon, they drove back into the District.* For locations within the District, use the geographical quadrant and *Washington: a Northeast Washington man*, (*not a Northeast D.C. man*), *the streets of Southwest Washington*. See also ADDRESSES. To distinguish it from the Washington, D.C., area, the state is Washington state.

weapons and weapons systems

The names of weapons and military aircraft are hyphenated when a hyphen appears in the official nomenclature: *F-15*, *B-1*, *C-5A*, *M-16 rifle*, *H-34 Choctaw helicopter*. In U.S. military terminology, the designation of an aircraft or "aerospace vehicle" is derived from its "basic mission symbol"—*F* for fighter, *B* for bomber, *H* for helicopter, *C* for cargo carrier—and its "design number." Under Pentagon regulations issued in 1976, the two are always separated by a hyphen. The Soviet Union also hyphenates: *AK-47*, *MiG-21*. For civilian aircraft, follow the manufacturer's designation: *Boeing 757*, *Tu-144* etc. When in doubt, consult Jane's All the World's Aircraft.

weightlifter, weightlifting*

weights and measures

See NUMERALS and DIMENSIONS.

welfare

Be careful to distinguish among applicants, cases, claimants, individuals, families, households and recipients—particularly when dealing with statistics.

Welsh rabbit

Not Welsh rarebit.

were

A clause introduced by *if* requires the subjunctive form *were* when it is contrary to fact or in expressions of doubt or regret: *If wishes were horses, beggars would ride. I wish it were possible to start over.* If it is not contrary to fact, or if it is not known whether it is contrary to fact, use *was*. *He asked if it was raining, because if it was they would have had to cancel the picnic. It wasn't. If it were, they would have had to cancel the picnic.*

wheelchair
See DISABLED.

whence
It means from where or from which. *From whence* is redundant.

whereabouts
With one person or a collective noun, the word is singular. *His whereabouts is unknown. The gang's whereabouts is unknown.* With more than one person, it is plural. *Their whereabouts are unknown.*

which
See THAT.

whiskey
But Scotch whisky.

who, whom
Who is used as a subject. *Whom* is used as the object of a verb or a preposition. *Who is going? The woman who did this should be punished. Whom did he meet there? To whom did you give it?* Some difficulty seems to arise in relative clauses containing the verb *say* or other attribution. But the rule does not change. *The suspect, who police said was armed, fled into the forest.* (*Who* is the subject of *was armed*). *The suspect, whom police described as armed and dangerous, fled into the forest.* (*whom* is the object of *described*.)

widow

A widow is a woman whose husband has died. Do not say *widow of the late* . . . In obituaries, a man is survived by his wife, not his widow.

willy-nilly

This expression means *whether the subject wants to or not*. It does not mean helter-skelter or at random. The expression is a corruption of the Latin *volens-nolens*, willing or unwilling.

wind chill index

Or wind chill equivalent—not factor. The wind chill index describes the combined effect of wind and cold temperature.

wind up (verb); *windup* (noun)

wine

Follow dictionary style on the names of wines and wine grapes: *zinfandel*, *Burgundy*, *Muscadet*, *pinot noir*. The names of vineyards and winemakers are proper names and are capitalized: *Chateau Greysac, a Marques de Riscal rioja*.

*working woman, working women**

World Bank

The official name is International Bank for Reconstruction and Development. World Bank is acceptable on all references.

World War I, World War II

yesterday

Do not use in datelined stories. Use the day of the week.

Zip code*

CHAPTER 6

REFERENCE GUIDE

Every large newspaper has its own library, usually staffed by a professional research librarian who is familiar with all the standard sources of information and data, such as the Statistical Abstract of the United States, the Merck Manual of Diagnosis and Therapy, Current Biography etc. The brief listing that follows is intended to help writers and editors who may need guidance on using the language and access on short notice to vital information about topics frequently in the news.

The Washington Post's authority on matters of spelling, punctuation and definition is Webster's New World Dictionary of American English (Third Edition), published in 1988. For additional guidance on usage questions, see also:

The Associated Press Stylebook and Libel Manual (Rev. ed., 1987). This contains especially useful sections on business and financial terms and on computer language.

The Oxford Guide to the English Language (Oxford: Oxford University Press, 1984).

Dictionary of Problem Words and Expressions, by Harry Shaw (New York: McGraw-Hill, Rev. ed., 1987).

American Heritage Dictionary of the English Language (American Heritage, 1969). This is the only general dictionary that pays particular attention to usage. Capsule comments prepared by a panel of writers, speakers and educators are scattered through the entries. Where there is a conflict in spelling or capitalization between the American Heritage Dictionary and Webster's New World, Webster's prevails in The Washington Post.

The Careful Writer: A Modern Guide to English Usage, by Theodore M. Bernstein (New York: Atheneum, 1965).

Chicago Manual of Style (Chicago: University of Chicago Press, 13th ed., 1982). This is definitive on matters of punctuation.

Dictionary of Contemporary Usage, by William Morris and Mary Morris (New York: Harper & Row, 1975).

Dictionary of Modern English Usage, by H.W. Fowler (Oxford: Oxford University Press, 2nd ed., 1965).

Dictionary of Contemporary Slang, by Jonathon Green (New York: Stein & Day, 1985).

Dictionary of Cliches, by James Rogers (New York: Facts on File, 1985).

On other topics, in addition to such standard sources as the World Almanac and the Who's Who series, the following specialized reference books are useful:

I.   Government and politics

Official Congressional Directory, the definitive guide to Congress and the federal government (published for each session of Congress by the Government Printing Office).

United States Government Manual, official handbook of the U.S. government (published by the office of the Federal Register, National Archives and Records Administration).

Federal Regulatory Directory for executive branch departments outside the Cabinet (published by Congressional Quarterly).

Almanac of American Politics, an authoritative guide to electoral politics (published every two years by National Journal).

II.   Weapons, aircraft and ships

The standard reference sources on military equipment and ships are the yearbooks of the Jane's series, published in London by Jane's Information Group. Among the volumes are Fighting Ships; All the World's Aircraft; Infantry Weapons; Weapon Systems; Armour and Artillery; and Air-Launched Weapons. See also "The Military Balance" (published annually by the International Institute of Strategic Studies in London), an invaluable source of information about the armed forces of every country.

III.   Religion

For data on church membership and organization, see the Yearbook of American and Canadian Churches. Also useful, especially on historical questions, is the New Catholic Encyclopedia.

IV.   International affairs

The Europa Yearbook (published annually by Europa Publications, London), contains reliable data on the geography, history, economy, government and politics of every foreign nation. The Statesman's Yearbook (published annually by Macmillan), is similar. Also valuable is the World Factbook (published annually by the Central Intelligence Agency). It gives the vital statistics, such as railroad mileage and life expectancy, for every country. On military matters, see "The Military Balance," listed in II, above.

V.   Music

The standard reference work is the New Grove Dictionary of Music and Musicians (New York: Macmillan, 1980). See also the Encyclopedia of Folk, Country and Western Music and the Encyclopedia of Pop, Rock and Soul (both published by St. Martin's Press).

VI.   Business and the economy

Consult Standard & Poor's Register of Corporations, Directors and Executives for information about corporations. For information and current statistics about business trends, trade and the economy, see the Survey of Current Business (published monthly by the Government Printing Office). According to Catherine A. Jones, chief of the congressional reference division of the Library of Congress, this is "the single most important statistical periodical published by the federal government." See also the Federal Reserve Bulletin (published monthly).

VII.   Publications

The most comprehensive listing of newspapers and magazines published in the United States is the Gale Directory of Publications (formerly known as the Ayer Directory). Published by Gale Research Co. of Detroit, it gives the names of each newspaper and magazine's executives and editors, addresses, circulation figures, publication schedule etc. The Editor and Publisher Yearbook contains similar data.

VIII. Crime

The Sourcebook of Criminal Justice Statistics (published annually by the Government Printing Office) contains more than statistics on crime. It includes regional data, statistics on prisons, lists of illegal goods seized, sentencing data etc.

IX. Law and lawyers

Black's Law Dictionary (West Publishing Co., St. Paul, Minn.) gives the definitions of all legal terms, ancient and modern. The Martindale-Hubbell Law Directory (published annually by Martindale-Hubbell, Summit, N.J.) lists lawyers, law firms and some of their clients, background on senior partners etc.

X. Medicine and science

The McGraw-Hill Dictionary of Scientific and Technical Terms is a comprehensive dictionary of the language of science. It gives authoritative definitions of tens of thousands of words used in the physical, natural and medical sciences. The Merck Manual of Diagnosis and Therapy (published by Merck & Co., the pharmaceutical company), is considered reliable on questions of medicine and treatment. Also useful is the Handbook of Chemistry and Physics (revised annually, published by Chemical Rubber Co., Cleveland). It has a good index to topics in the chemical and physical sciences.

INDEX